Works Team

The Rootes Competition Department

Works Team

The Rootes Competition Department

Michael Frostick

ISBN 0 9530721 1 8

Published by
Mercian Manuals, Coventry.
242 Station Road,
Coventry CV7 7EE

Foreword

I must make it quite clear from the outset that this book is not complete—if by complete you mean that nothing has been left out. It seems likely that at least as much has been omitted as has been included, and even the records at the end of the book are not exhaustive. For example, if you won the Honeycomb Rally in 1957 in a Sunbeam Alpine, the sad truth is that there is unlikely to be a record of the fact in these pages.

There is, however, a reason for this; the complete list, if it were possible to assemble such a thing, would occupy six volumes instead of one and, apart from its very doubtful use as a record for posterity, it would probably be the most boring book ever published.

I have tried, therefore, to provide a concise history of the development of the Rootes competition department which while frankly missing some things out succeeds nevertheless in telling the story and giving the reader, in readable terms, an idea of what went on and why.

There can be no doubt that it is an exciting tale, a demonstration, if ever one was needed, of the way in which a well-run competition department helps with the development of the production car. It is also a tribute, as it rightly should be, to the ability and tenacity of Norman Garrad, who built this department from one grudgingly provided side-valve Sunbeam-Talbot to the important place it holds in the British motor industry today.

I am as usual indebted to any number of people for help in assembling this work. Obviously, mostly to members of the Rootes Organisation; particularly to Norman Garrad himself; his son Lewis; to George Hartwell who played no small part in this story; to John Wilcox and John Rowe of the Press department—the latter having also done service as team manager; and to the indefatigable and charming Jeannette Wilkinson, the librarian of the public relations department. I am also indebted through Mrs Wilkinson to the late Jackie Masters who, although he was in hospital, provided from his files all manner of treasures.

Outside the Group and going further back, I am much indebted to Georges Roesch, who talks endlessly, for talking endlessly about the STD empire; also to the Royal Automobile Club in the person of Pat Gregory for permission to use the RAC library, and to Lord Montagu and my other friends at Beaulieu for their usual willing assistance.

Contents

chapter 1 **Antecedents**

It has been said that the complexities of the Sunbeam-Talbot-Darracq combine were greater than those of the Holy Roman Empire, and it is doubtful if Charlemagne could really give much on points to Louis Coatalen at Sunbeams. The Talbot was a

S.P. Mills, winner of the 1907 Heavy Tourist Trophy Race at the wheel of the Beeston Humber, with his mechanic, J. Swift. The erection behind the front seats was part of the handicapping system designed to produce limousine-type wind resistance

rather more English dog and one is driven to Arthurian com-
parisons—certainly for a mixture of genius and sheer cussedness
Merlin himself had nothing on Roesch. However, the names of
Sunbeam and Talbot were not joined until 1919, when the industry
began to re-form itself after the First World War—and then it was
nearly twenty years before these twins were absorbed into the
Rootes Organisation.

The Sunbeam Company had enjoyed very considerable competition success before the First World War and in 1913 a Talbot
driven by Percy Lambert became the first car to cover 100 miles
in an hour. The car was in fact one of the four-cylinder 25·6 hp
models, which not only covered a flying half mile at 113·28 mph,
but covered 103 miles in sixty minutes.

The first Sunbeam car was built by Thomas Curreton at a
Wolverhampton cycle works in 1899. With a single-cylinder
engine, belt transmission and wooden wheels, it was an unlikely-
looking sire for the family portrayed in this book. However, ten
years later, hot-foot from his success with the Humber and
Hillman companies (the arm of coincidence is indeed long), came
Louis Coatalen to design the 16/20 hp model which was to prove

'Toodles II' with Louis Coatalen at the wheel

so successful that a year later the Sunbeam works had to be enlarged to deal with the volume of orders.

Coatalen was an enthusiast and within a year was hard at work producing a strange assortment of Sunbeam racing cars, most of which were rendered the more curious by such names as 'Nautilus' and 'Toodles II'. By 1912 Coatalen had persuaded his not unwilling masters to commit themselves to the racing game and at Dieppe in 1912 a team of three 12/16 hp Sunbeams finished in the first three places in the Coupe de l'Auto, while in the Grand Prix itself they managed to be third, fourth and fifth.

The following year with a new 30 hp model Sunbeams went to Brooklands and captured all the world's records from one to twelve hours and from fifty to 100 miles. The drivers for this marathon were none other than Kenelm Lee Guinness, Chassagne and a gentleman by the name of Resta, whose fame seems not to have survived like that of his co-drivers. The following year Coatalen produced a special 30 hp twelve-cylinder car which gained the world speed record at 120·73 mph and, competition being fierce, Coatalen took a good look at the overhead camshaft Peugeots and produced for the Tourist Trophy a car good enough to let Lee Guinness win the event. By this time the war clouds had gathered and competition motoring, both in terms of engineering and human derring-do, was transferred to the Royal Flying Corps, which in turn gave birth to the RAF.

With the return to peace and the hammering of swords into ploughshares, the motor industry found itself immensely far forward in terms of technology. With a sellers' market beating on its doors for anything on wheels which might go from London to Brighton, or at least as far down that already busy road as the first reasonable hostelry, it was an age of opportunity—and Coatalen was nothing if not an opportunist. The Sunbeam-Talbot-Darracq combine emerged; and the great days of motor sport stood by for time to turn a page and a new exciting chapter to begin.

Coatalen's post-war formula produced some of the most colourful achievements in British motoring history. It was at this time that he produced the great Sunbeam record-breaking cars, mostly fitted with 18·3-litre Coatalen-designed aero engines—a V12 with an overhead camshaft for each bank of cylinders. With this engine he achieved not only the fastest time at the Gaillon Hillclimb, but also took the land speed record at Brooklands when the car driven by Kenelm Lee Guinness managed either 137·15 mph or 140·4 mph, depending upon whose results you happen to read. In any event, Malcolm Campbell then bought the car, took it to Pendine Sands and, after participating in what are probably

Malcolm Campbell and mechanics at Pendine, 21 July 1925

the most nauseating set of publicity photographs ever offered to
the national Press, succeeded in raising the world land speed
record to slightly over 150 mph. This was in 1922.

From 1923 onwards, with the assistance of Henry O'Neal
Dehane Segrave, the Bertarione-designed Grand Prix cars, which
were undoubtedly the fastest racing cars in Europe at that time,
won not only the French Grand Prix but also the Spanish Grand
Prix, and Segrave thus anticipated Moss by some thirty-five or
more years. Renewed attacks on the land speed record were then
made, first with a diminutive 4-litre twelve-cylinder car and then
with the immortal Red Monster in which Segrave at Daytona
raised the world land speed record to over 200 mph. This car,
which is now preserved in the Montagu Motor Museum at
Beaulieu, was the famous '1,000 Horsepower' machine of vast
proportions and tank-like appearance (in which by imitation it

*A photograph taken at San Sebastian showing H.M. King Alfonso of
Spain and the late Sir Henry Segrave*

Segrave at Southport with the 4-litre Sunbeam, March 1926

The Red Monster being uncrated at the Clarendon Garage, Daytona Beach, Florida, by the seven mechanics who accompanied the car from Wolverhampton (1927)

flattered both Voisin and Bugatti) driven by two Sunbeam Matabele V12 aero engines each of 22½-litre capacity, the cooling arrangements of which were such that the redoubtable Segrave had to be encased in an armour-plated cockpit lest he should burn up himself before he burned up the record. The car itself weighed nearly four tons and was nearly twenty-four feet long; the engines each reputedly of 500 hp were mounted fore and aft of the driving seat on a channel steel chassis frame.

By the time the glory of this effort had subsided and Segrave had received his knighthood, Coatalen had tired of English cooking

The official note by the RAC steward and timekeeper of the times achieved by Major Segrave on the 4-litre Sunbeam at Southport, 16 March 1926. The attempt on the mile record failed because of a defect in the casing of the supercharger

Divo and Hivernat on No. 7 Sunbeam during the French Grand Prix at Tours, 1923

Segrave at San Sebastian, 25 July 1926

and left for Paris. With his departure went the greatness of the Sunbeam production at Wolverhampton—the famous twin-cam 3-litre went out of production and although fine cars continued to be produced, the mantle of greatness in the strange STD empire which was to father the present Rootes competition department descended upon the ebullient and enigmatic Swiss, Georges Roesch, and it was not long after this that Norman Garrad, who might well be described as the godfather of the outfit, came into the picture.

Roesch had started work in the late autumn of 1925 on the production of the 14/45 Talbot that appeared at the 1926 Motor

Coatalen and Segrave with the Mayor of Wolverhampton on the occasion of a public luncheon to Segrave, 27 April 1927

A private entrant: G. H. Jackson, 3-litre eight-cylinder Sunbeam, 10-mile race Southport, July 1926

Show with a price tag of £395. The 14/45 was a large car available as an immense and sedate open tourer or as an even more immense and even more sedate fabric saloon. Its top gear ratio was as low as 5·87 : 1 and it was without sporting pretensions. Indeed, only a brave few of its owners worked it up to the modest maximum of 65 mph to find out how sweet and smooth its power unit was at that 'excessive' speed. In 1929 Roesch offered the 75; it had the same 'knitting needle' pushrods, but a new seven-bearing counterbalanced crankshaft, while the bore and stroke were up from the 61 × 95 mm of the original car to 69·5 × 100, giving a capacity of 2,276 cc. In no time at all Roesch had produced a better model still with the 90, in which he had dramatically raised the compression ratio to 10 : 1—and then the fun began!

In 1930, the year in which Coatalen returned to France, Roesch achieved first, second and third places in the Irish Grand Prix, the RAC Tourist Trophy and the Brooklands 500-mile race, while Brian Lewis slipped silently and swiftly into third place at Le Mans behind the massive 6½-litre Bentleys and ahead of Lord Howe's 1,750 Alfa Romeo, an effort described by Charles Faroux as 'absolutely stupefying'.

In 1931 the 105 model was introduced complete with Wilson pre-selector gearbox, which even in its standard production form had a maximum speed of over 95 mph and was capable of accelerating from 0 to 50 in ten seconds. A team of these cars with open Vanden Plas bodies—tourers—won the 1932 Coupe des Alpes and was in fact the first British team to do so since 1914. It was incidentally the first British team to complete this strenuous international alpine trial without the loss of a single mark, and it is not without note, as far as this volume is concerned, to recall that car No. 9 was driven by Norman Garrad. In 1933 Talbots rested on their laurels, but in 1934 a team of 105s, this time fitted with the less beautiful but more efficient 'racing' bodies, repeated the 1932 success, driven by Tommy Wisdom/Mrs Wisdom, H. Eaton/B. B. Higgins and W. M. Couper/G. Day. Higgins was a works mechanic and Day was Talbots' chief tester. This policy of employing works personnel on the more adventurous competition sorties is one which Norman Garrad has perpetuated.

But once more the shadows of war loomed on the horizon and

The team of Talbot '105' models which won the Coupe des Alpes in the 1932 Alpine Rally. This was the first time for eighteen years that a British team had won the Coupe; they repeated their success in 1934. Left to right: Hon. Brian Lewis (now Lord Essendon), 'Tim' Rose-Richards and Norman Garrad

the financial situation was such that the Sunbeam-Talbot-Darracq empire began to crumble.

It is at this point that the Rootes Group enters the story, and it can hardly be expected to do so unannounced. The Rootes brothers began their career in the motor trade when, as partners, they built up a flourishing car sales business in Kent shortly after the First World War. Later they moved to Long Acre and shortly after that, in 1926, they took over the premises in Devonshire House, Piccadilly, which have remained their headquarters ever since.

They made their reputation and built their business on the selling of motor cars and by 1928 they were the largest distributors in England, and it was at that point that they crossed their biggest bridge and decided to become motor manufacturers by acquiring control of the Humber, Hillman and Commer companies.

These companies at that time were handicapped by outdated plant and old-fashioned production methods and the success of the Rootes Group lay then, even as it does now, in the rationalization of production. Later they acquired Karrier Motors and in 1935 Clement Talbot Ltd came under the control of Rootes Securities. British Light Steel Pressings followed in 1937 and a year later the Sunbeam Motor Company was taken into the Rootes Group and merged with Clement Talbot. In point of fact, Rootes had had a good hand in Sunbeam finances for some years before that.

The acquisition of the Singer company did not occur until the end of December 1955. It could perhaps be argued that the early successes of Singer cars in competition—particularly the famous Le Mans Singer—have some place in these antecedents, but in fact Singer's role as a competition car had ceased some time before they became part of the Rootes Organisation and there do not, therefore, seem to be any really substantial grounds for their inclusion.

To go back to the period before the Second World War, we find Sunbeams and Talbots both out of production in the ordinary sense of the word, and a new range of models, originally called Talbot and subsequently named Sunbeam-Talbot, on the market using everything but the body from the Humber/Hillman range. In 1957 the marque name reverted to just 'Sunbeam'. It was not until Norman Garrad was released from the Forces after the war that the challenge was once more taken up and the true beginning of the story which this book seeks to tell came about.

chapter 2 **1946-1949**

1. THE 2-LITRE SIDE VALVE

In the months immediately after the war the entire motor industry enjoyed a game of general post of hitherto undreamed-of proportions. While the actual product was undergoing a process of being transformed (once again!) from a sword blade to a plough-share, the people responsible for production were not only playing musical chairs but changing horses in mid-stream as well. Donald Healey and Sampietro had been working with the Rootes Group during the war and had admitted that during their long periods of fire-watching they had been dreaming up a sports car. By the time dreams might have been expected to become reality these two had gone off elsewhere and about the only figure with any interest in competitions to be seen in the Ryton-on-Dunsmore area was Norman Garrad, who had just been demobbed after spending the last few years in the 3rd Armoured Division as a Lieutenant-Colonel.

At this time, in common with everybody else, the Rootes Group were trying to get back into production and were naturally enough manufacturing in 1946 and 1947 the same motor cars as they had been making before the war, so that in order to continue our story it is now necessary to go back to 1939, if not before.

When the Rootes Group took over the old Talbot Company they horrified a number of purists by producing a Talbot 10 which was clearly based on the then current Aero-Minx. By 1938 the car had grown into a four-door model of very attractive appearance and almost non-existent performance. The period of the small Six had passed, but the doctrine of a lot of engine in a little car was beginning to make itself felt on the Continent and British manufacturers were certainly toying with the idea as a marketable proposition. In the late summer of 1939 (in preparation for a Motor Show which never took place) Rootes announced that the Sunbeam Talbot 10 would also be available as a 2-litre—which meant in fact that they were putting into it the engine from what was then known as the Hillman 14 (a car which shared its body-pressing with the Humber Super Snipe—*plus ça change. . .*) . The car went on the market at £315 and a week or two later the market came to a full stop.

In 1945 the car reappeared at £625, which was only about double; and this price was inflated by the Chancellor of the Exchequer to £799 7s. 2d. by the imposition of purchase tax. A year later the total price had risen to £927 2s. 9d. The sellers' market was in full force, the world of motoring competition had hardly begun to stir from its seven-year sleep and motor manu-facturers were not as a whole in any way interested in adding to their burdens by the creation of a competition department.

Norman Garrad, however, was not the kind of person to take 'no' for an answer and although his efforts to lay his hands on one

Probably not as fast as the royal Daimler in the background, the 2-litre side-valve Sunbeam-Talbot was nevertheless the foundation-stone upon which Norman Garrad built the Competition Department

of the 2-litre cars to use in competition were seen by the engineering department to be nothing more nor less than a desire to break
up a perfectly good motor car, and by the sales department as
the waste of a vehicle which might otherwise have been sold for
profit, he did in fact succeed in getting hold of one of the saloon
versions in order to 'cover' the Alpine Rally of that year for the
Rootes Group magazine *Modern Motoring and Travel*.

The car did not in fact have a very good performance, giving
road test figures of between 72 and 76 mph. The 2-litre engine,
however, which developed 56 bhp from 1,944 cc (instead of 41 bhp
from 1,185 in the so-called '10') was not overworked as the car
was fairly light, and at least the *Autocar* was able to praise its
cable-operated brakes. Garrad, however, came back with a rather
different report, to the effect that the car was 'exceedingly
dangerous' to drive fast down the mountain passes because of
serious brake-fade. He was able to add that the shock absorbers
had lasted but two and a half hours, that the fuel vaporized in the
pipe lines, that the tyres gave trouble and that the gear ratios were
unsuitable. He added to this the alarming information that after
three or four hairpins the steering became so stiff that it required
all the force he could muster to turn the steering wheel at all!

Lesser men might have given Garrad his cards and left it at that,
but in fact the engineering department under its director, Bernard
Winter, listened with some sympathy to what Garrad had to say.
Brake lining manufacturers were consulted and Mintex produced
the M.20 lining after various different brake drums, even those of
increased diameter, had effected only a partial cure. Similar
experiment was carried on with the shock absorber settings, petrol
pipes were moved to avoid the heat of the exhaust and the gearbox
was re-designed to give better-spaced ratios. Stromberg coped with
the problems of carburation at high altitudes and new anti-friction
materials were introduced for the steering pivots when every other
effort failed to improve the situation. This work, of course,
continued over a period of months and much of it did not
benefit the motoring public until the new model was announced
in June 1948.

2. THE INTRODUCTION OF THE OHV MODELS

The new ohv models, known as the 80 and 90 (to quote the
Motor Year Book—'a return to the nomenclature popular on
Talbot models some years ago'), were introduced in June 1948
when a heavier but much more attractive body was offered. The

chassis was very much the same as that on the previous cars, still using semi-elliptic front springs and a solid front axle. The engines had new cast-iron overhead valve cylinder heads but were still fundamentally the original Hillman 14/Hillman Minx engines. It is interesting to note that although the heads were of similar design, they were fitted the opposite way round on the two different engines, the 80 having its camshaft on the offside and the 90 on the nearside. Karslake and Ian Nickols in their famous book *Motoring Entente* have suggested that this fact might be turned into a good round song—something perhaps for Flanders and Swann when they drop yet another hat. The 90 or 2-litre engine was now persuaded to give 64 bhp, an increase of 14·3 per cent over the previous model, and although, as we have said, the weight was increased, it was much less than the increase in power so that a considerable margin of improvement was shown in the overall performance. The cars had Lockheed hydraulic brakes with two leading shoes (to make Garrad feel safer on the mountains) and as a direct result of the competition experience the Stromberg carburettors had fresh air led to them from a separate intake beside the radiator, providing a supply of cold air, thereby eliminating some of the difficulties previously experienced with high under-bonnet temperatures under extreme operating conditions which had complicated carburation problems and reduced efficiency by lowering the charge weight in the earlier models. Special LOEX light-alloy pistons were provided which even went so far as to have a vacant groove in the skirt for an extra ring should additional oil control become necessary after long service. The chassis was strengthened and the steering improved and the price was put up by £50.

The car was hardly off the drawing board before Murray Frame took a Coupe des Alpes in one of the new 90 models. Garrad and Horton also competed in the same event, but damaged the sump of their car so seriously that the crankshaft could be heard battering against it. It need hardly be said that future production models had stronger sumps and from then on sump protectors were a *sine qua non* of competition cars.

While this rather simple beginning to the competition story may seem to lack glamour, Garrad had proved beyond a shadow of doubt that participation in this kind of competition invariably produced answers which were not available from any other source, and while the new cars were fundamentally the same mechanically as the immediate post-war models, they were in fact much improved and the addition of the new bodies was not simply the pouring of old wine into new bottles.

By this time the authorities at Rootes—which really means the family (it is still a family business and a very enlightened one at that)—were beginning to appreciate the dividends which the expenditure in the competition department was producing and in 1948 the cars were first seriously entered in competition, a team of three 80 models being run in the 1949 Monte Carlo Rally, the cars being driven by Peter Monkhouse, Nick Haines and George Hartwell. Monkhouse, fourth in the 1,500 cc class, was thirty-first overall; Haines with Leslie Johnson and John Eason Gibson as co-drivers thirty-seventh, and Hartwell forty-sixth.

Gatsonides also appeared at the wheel of a Rootes product, driving a Hillman Minx into nineteenth place. The weather was on the whole rather good, the major hazard in the event being the festivities held at Boulogne by the civic authorities which more or less forcibly delayed a large number of the Glasgow contingent so that many of them arrived late at Luxembourg. There was a regularity run over a rather difficult course after the arrival at Monte Carlo, and although in the words of a contemporary report 'Sunbeam-Talbots were driven with great urge by Monkhouse, Haines and Johnson', they did not in fact do particularly well.

Success began to crown their efforts in the summer of that year when a team of three 90s was entered in the Alpine Rally and came away with a special award for the best non-French team. In fact, they won the prize 'as the only eligible marque with three cars intact', Citroëns having won the team prize proper. All the same, the cars had shown up well despite this not particularly charitable comment by Joseph Lowrey in the *Motor* for in fact Monkhouse and Hartwell, who Lowrey says 'were consistently getting their Sunbeam-Talbot far ahead of its team mates', finished fifth overall with Douglas Clease of the *Autocar* twentieth and Norman Garrad himself twenty-fifth.

The cars again appeared in the 1950 Monte Carlo Rally and Peter Monkhouse once more put up the best performance in the team. Unfortunately, he could manage no more than forty-sixth, Garrad and Cutts being sixty-sixth and Pearman and Chipperton sixty-eighth. However, Rootes' position this year was much improved by Gatsonides, this time achieving second place in a Humber Super Snipe—and indeed he nearly won the event, losing it by a hair's breadth on the Mont des Mules regularity test. Also, as if to carry on the pre-war Sunbeam and Talbot tradition, a Hillman Minx was judged the best-equipped car in the Rally. This year there were something more like true Monte Carlo Rally conditions in that there was a good deal of snow and ice, and

Beginning a long climb near Cortina. Mile after mile in third, perhaps second gear, is a test for any gearbox

even if the team did not do all that well, they were beginning to flex their muscles and find out what it was all about.

Fate took a turn against the team later on that year when Monkhouse died tragically while acting as a passenger in the Mille Miglia. However, the resourceful Garrad was quick to secure the services of Maurice Gatsonides, who had done so well in the 'Monte', and so it was Gatsonides who led the team in the 1950 Alpine, backed up by Hartwell and Murray Frame. Gatsonides and Hartwell were first and second respectively in the 2-litre class at half distance; but the overall result was not as happy as all that.

There had been a considerable fuss at the beginning of the Rally since the scrutineers had decided to enforce the regulations instead of turning a perpetual blind eye, and many of the competitors were unable to start. Here the Rootes Group's professional approach to rallying began to pay dividends in that the cars were what they purported to be, and no real trouble was experienced. In the event Murray Frame had extremely bad luck since he had made every control on time and would have won a Coupe des Alpes but for the fact that his starter motor failed at Monte Carlo and cost him five marks. In fact, his battery had gone the night before and he had only been kept in the Rally by the whole team stopping from time to time and swopping their batteries round (an example of team management at its best). Garrad had been delayed by bits falling off the car and Gatsonides had broken his back axle. Hartwell was involved in a collision and although he stayed at the scene of the accident to help sort it out he was not allowed to pass through the frontier as were most of the Rally, and indeed was fired at with pistols when he tried. As if that was not trouble enough, his dynamo came adrift. Tommy Wisdom appeared in that event, driving a Hillman Minx.

In September of that year the 80 model was dropped altogether and everything was concentrated on the 90. The front suspension was redesigned on independent lines and the gear ratio raised. In point of fact there were still a good many chassis at the factory with a solid front axle and this model remained on the home market for some months after the new one had been introduced 'for export only'. It made its first competition appearance in the Monte Carlo Rally of the following year, which brings us to the beginning of another chapter.

chapter 3 **The 80s and 90s**

In September 1950 the existing 90 was radically changed. The new car, known as the Sunbeam Talbot Mark II, was offered to the public with coachwork similar to that of the previous model, but with the bore increased from 75 to 81 mm to give no less than 2,267 cc, an increase in capacity of nearly $16\frac{1}{2}$ per cent; in fact, 70 bhp at 4,000 rpm instead of 64 bhp at 4,100. The power curves all showed a variable increase throughout the range, providing not only an increase in maximum speed but a distinct improvement in the performance at the bottom end of the graph as well as more effortless cruising on higher gear ratios. The general design and lay-out of the engine closely followed the former 1,944 cc unit, but incorporated minor improvements to the cooling system and to the oil-filling arrangements. The chassis frame was completely new and designed to provide increased rigidity for the newly introduced independent front suspension. This was of the coil type with upper and lower links of different lengths, the upper wishbones taking the form of welded pressings, while the lower links were forged steel frames braced by the pan which carried the coil spring. At the rear the underslung semi-elliptic springs were increased in length from forty-five inches to fifty-two inches and the width of the leaves from one and three-quarter inches to two inches, the net result of which was to provide a softer ride. However, no doubt bearing the requirements of the competition department in mind, a Panhard rod was added to the lay-out in order to ensure that the softer suspension should not interfere with lateral stability.

On the new model the steering was by a variable ratio Burman steering box of re-circulating ball type. A divided track rod was used via a drop arm with transverse rod and lever assembly pivoted to the centre of the main member carrying the suspension.

The new lay-out was higher geared than before. Again, perhaps with the Alpine Trial in mind, the body ventilation system was arranged to take fresh air from two small grilles which flanked the radiator in the position previously occupied by two fog lamps, and although very few people noticed the change the front wings were in fact re-styled so that the headlamps were three inches higher than before.

From the foregoing it can be seen that the car was now beginning to move into quite a different class and to become a serious competition contender; a *Motor* road test early in 1951 gave the maximum as 84·5 mph. And so we come back to the competition scene.

The new car made its début in the 1951 Monte Carlo Rally, in which Norman Garrad shared a car with Basil Cardew. Gatsonides won the prize for the best-equipped car and R. P. Minchin of the Metropolitan Police drove a Humber Super Snipe.

Garrad was away in the United States when the Alpine Trial came along, but Pearman and Cutts were third in their class despite having to compete with cars up to 3-litre.

The following year, 1952, the Rootes competition department, in conjunction with the firm generally, really took the bull by the

Hartwell on the Digne–Grasse section of the Monte, 1952

Stirling Moss—deep snow and the consequences

Stirling Moss and Mike Hawthorn at Northolt Airport on a dash to Silverstone, after having put up a fine performance in the Sunbeam Talbot team in the 1952 Alpine Rally. The team awards included three Coupes des Alpes, 1st, 2nd and 3rd in the 2–3 litre class and the manufacturers' team prize

horns and had what is probably their most successful year. The cars were further improved and known as the Mark IIA, incorporating many of the lessons that had been learned in the previous year's competition and, quite apart from the improvements which Rootes had been able to make themselves, they were now in a sufficiently strong position to demand that their component manufacturers should join in their quest for perfection. Dunlop were able to give enormous assistance with the introduction of the Dunlop 90 and Fort covers, Lucas worked hard to obviate dynamo and starter-motor failures caused by overheating due to lack of ventilation and breakage of mounting brackets, and indeed the introduction of the famous Lucas 'Flamethrower' was largely due to requests from the Rootes competition department. Their own engineering works had done much to get rid of the mechanical difficulties and had worked more or less continuously on the steering and front suspension which was by now much improved. They had also done a good deal to the oil system of the

Stirling Moss and the late John 'Autocar' Cooper preparing to start the 1952 Monte. Trousers have changed but the Hotel Metropole remains the same

engines since, just as the old Talbot 105s had done long before the war, they suffered from oil surge in the sump on the mountain passes. This had been dealt with by using a larger intake to the oil pump and re-arranging sump baffles.

Garrad now went straight to the top in his search to build a team worthy of the cars and persuaded both Stirling Moss and Mike Hawthorn to drive for him. Moss joined the team in time for the Monte Carlo Rally of 1952 and drove with the late John Cooper, who was at that time Sports Editor of the *Autocar*. This year it was a real 'Monte' with a vengeance, there being heavy snow almost throughout Europe and very fierce competition. Moss, who was not a practised Rally driver, put up the most astonishing performance, coming in to finish second overall in the Rally. It was a pity that this year coincided with Sidney Allard's great triumph in one of his own cars. A pity not because one would begrudge Allard his success but simply, at least from the point of view of this book, because that success overshadowed the beginnings of tremendous effort by Rootes. No one who saw

E. S. Sneath's Sunbeam-Talbot on a regularity test 1952 Monte Carlo Rally

Some of the works team in the Rallye des Alpes, including Mike Haw-thorn, Leslie Johnson and Stirling Moss

them would like to choose the better man; Allard was the rougher of the two, literally bouncing his car off walls of snow (and occasionally brick) to get round the special test in time—indeed, most of the marks he lost were for dents. Stirling was only a fraction slower but a great deal neater and the Rootes competition department was not faced with so much panel beating at the end of the event.

The full weight was then prepared for the forthcoming Alpine Trial. Once more Garrad followed his policy of having people from the works in the cars. Moss, who had already driven for Rootes in the Monte Carlo Rally, had as his co-driver John Cutts; 'Chips' Chipperton went with Hawthorn, who was still only what

3

the Continentals call a 'comingman', and John Pearman went with Murray Frame. By this time the competition department was in full swing and the cars were always modified specially for the event under the arrangements made in the competition department. Details of these 'preparation schedules' can be found in Appendix II at the end of the book, where they can more easily be studied than here in the middle of the story. Sufficient to say at this moment that not only were the drivers briefed on the route and every dodge made known to them, but every comfort was cared for by the provision of special seats giving proper support, special ventilation for both the engine and the driver, special lights and instruments and all the paraphernalia which we have since come to associate with competition cars of this kind.

The Rally itself was an extremely difficult one; the average speeds had been put up and the control points had been made closer together and the route not only included the ordinary French Alps but had a great deal of extraordinarily difficult

8,000 ft up; the team on a practice run near the summit of Mont Ventoux in the 1951 Alpine

Leslie Johnson and his co-driver David Humphrey negotiating Stelvo

territory in the Dolomites. Hartwell and Johnson were both eliminated on the first day between Bolzano and Cortina over the steep and difficult Pordoi Pass. John Fitch, the American racing driver who was also in a Sunbeam Talbot, had to retire when a hub bearing broke, and Nancy Mitchell, one of the first of Garrad's famous Girls, was within sixty miles of the finish when one of her front wheels collapsed. However, in the team proper Murray Frame and Pearman were placed eighth; Hawthorn and Chipperton ninth; Stirling Moss and Cutts tenth. At one point, incidentally, Moss lost twenty-six minutes trying to put his exhaust system back on the car and then made up the loss over one of the worst sections with a drive of which only Moss was capable, and the team remained intact to win three Coupes des Alpes, all the up to 3-litre class prizes, the manufacturers' team prize and another team prize known as the 'Challenge de l'Automobile Club de Marseille et Provence'. They were also first in the acceleration and braking test in the 2 to 3-litre class.

It was about this time that Sheila van Damm first came into the picture. She had in fact first been introduced to Garrad at the 1951 Motor Show. Impressed by her sincerity, Garrad offered her a car for the 1952 *Daily Express* Rally. Nothing particularly sensational came from this, but Miss van Damm finished third in the Ladies' Class, even though no one had given her any special tuition for the tests, and Tommy Wisdom noticed that try as he might he failed to shake her off on any of the longer and more exciting sections. And so she joined the team for the following year.

Garrad's Follies! (In a theatrical sense.) 1954 Monte Carlo Rally—Sheila van Damm, Anne Hall and Françoise Clarke

We cannot, however, close a report of 1952 without taking note
of the fact that the Sunbeam Talbot team were awarded the
RAC Dewar Trophy for the most outstanding engineering and
technical achievements of the year; and that Stirling Moss and
Leslie Johnson drove a Super Snipe from Oslo to Lisbon—
fifteen countries in five days.

The year 1953 sees the mixture as before. Sheila van Damm
drove a Hillman Minx with Mrs Bill Wisdom and Mrs Fothering-
ham-Parker. Their failure to understand the jacking system cost
them the Ladies' Prize and Sheila's enthusiasm nearly went too
far when she strained herself rather badly trying to hold the car up
while the others changed the wheel when they could not make the
jack work! A Sunbeam Talbot won the Concours de Confors and
they won the team prize for the best performance by any three
nominated cars—the first time that a British make had won this
trophy (the Charles Faroux Cup) for twenty-one years.

THE FIRST 'ALPINE'

In March of this year (1953), no doubt partly as a result of
Garrad's visit to America, Rootes were persuaded to offer an
open two-seater for the first time, the idea being to offer an
attractive-looking car using the engine and chassis which had done

*Drivers with Stirling Moss in the Fifteen Countries in Five Days: Leslie
Johnson, John Coutts and David Humphrey (see Appendix VI)*

Mock-up of the first Sunbeam Alpine by George Hartwell Ltd of Bournemouth

so well in the saloon. In order to increase its performance the compression ratio was raised from 6·45 : 1 to 7·42 : 1. The valve guides were shortened and the ports modified so that the power output was raised from 70 bhp at 4,000 rpm to 80 bhp at 4,200 rpm. Other modifications included a single Stromberg DAA36 downdraught carburettor, a Burgess straight-through silencer, a Lucas high-voltage sports coil with manual control, a deeper radiator block, stiffer coil springs, a larger anti-roll bar and harder settings for the R-type Armstrong shock absorbers. Gear ratios were changed to give higher speeds in the indirect ratios, but the maximum speed remained rather less than 100 miles an hour, mostly because of the weight which was still high owing to the necessity for welding side plates to the frame and fitting a two-inch tubular cross-member below the engine—such is the price that must be paid when you take the lid off the box.

To give the car a proper send-off, an expedition was made to the then recently opened motorway in Belgium known at that time as the Jabbeke Highway, because this was the name of the village where the thing petered out when it ought to have gone on to Ostend. For this expedition a special car was produced with further modifications including a metal undershield which greatly

Stirling Moss and Sheila van Damm at Jabbeke

Garrad, Moss, Johnson, Sheila van Damm and onlookers, Montlhéry, immediately after the runs at Jabbeke. 111·20 miles in an hour

Line-up: no prizes for identifying the drivers

improved the streamlining at the expense of accessibility. Sheila
van Damm drove it at 120·125 mph over a flying kilometre, and
although Stirling Moss was in attendance this fine run by Miss
van Damm stood as the record. Leslie Johnson then took the car
to Montlhéry and covered 111·20 miles in an hour and Moss did
a couple of laps at 116 mph. The newspapers covered the event
and the advertisers made the most of it. A good deal of the credit
for this development should in fact go to David Hodkin who,
while working for Leslie Johnson at ERA, had done most of the
work.

It is an interesting sideline that in an effort to keep the engine
cool a series of experiments was conducted on airflow, not, as one
might imagine, scientifically in a wind tunnel, but by the simple
expedient of holding a feather duster on the bonnet. This revealed,
among other things, that very little hot air came out of the louvres

cut in the top and so trap doors *à la* Citroën were incorporated in the sides of the bonnet, which prove very efficacious.

While all this was going on the final apotheosis of the old Sunbeam-Talbot was taking place. For reasons connected with the export market (and the introduction of the new model) the name Talbot was dropped—in any event, Tony Largo's French company was still functioning—and the new saloon was known as the Sunbeam Mark III. This had its compression ratio raised to $7.42 : 1$ (using the head evolved for the Alpine) and gave 77 bhp at 4,100 rpm—nearly 95 miles an hour. All this was extremely creditable and the Press was unanimous in its praise of the great improvements to suspension, steering and road holding which had been effected over the previous seven years, nearly all

Monte Carlo Rally 1955: the winning Sunbeam driven by Per Malling and Gunnar Fadum. Not only our *policemen are wonderful*

of which were due one way or another to the efforts of the
competition department. Nevertheless, the car had been developed
on the old principle of having a chassis and a body and these
improvements had only been achieved by adding strengthening
pieces at every convenient (and one or two inconvenient) places,
so that the car in fact weighed nearly twenty-six hundredweight
and still had only a modest amount of room for four people. The
real answer to this, of course, was to make a new car based on
the Monocoque principle, which is exactly what the company did,
having achieved four Coupes des Alpes and the Coupe des Dames
in the Alpine Rally, won the team prize in the Great American
Mountain Rally, the Coupe des Dames in the RAC and a smashing
outright victory in the Alpine Rally of Australia. It might be ob-
served that not only the Alpine but also the Alps were catching
on! The Mark III Sunbeam in fact continued in use as the
competition car throughout 1954 and 1955 and a list of its successes can be found on page 87. Not the least of these victories

1954 Monte—Garrad and Johnson (and not only trousers. See p. 23)

1954 Alpine Rally: Sheila van Damm and Anne Hall climb the Vivione.
In places the track is only just wide enough for a car to get through

was that of the Norwegians Per Malling and Gunnar Fadum;
'amateurs' who won the Monte Carlo Rally outright in 1955. The
Mark III made its last appearance in the Monte Carlo Rally of
1956, the Rapier taking over not only the next chapter but the
Mille Miglia of that year.

chapter 4 # The Rapier—the First Thrust

It seems to be a perennial truth in the motor trade that one thing leads to another and if you are going to be honest about the Sunbeam Rapier you have to start with a rather squashy Hillman Minx of the type that Sheila van Damm had driven some while previously. This car, an admirable family model, which had shown up fairly well in competition whenever it had been used, was available not only as a saloon but also as a drophead coupé, or convertible if you prefer the expression, with a body made by Carbodies. At some point in its career, and no doubt with the American market in mind, somebody had conceived the idea of putting a non-detachable hard top on this body—a practice already rife across the Atlantic—and so the Hillman Californian was produced. While it may be argued that the first Sunbeam Rapier was a very considerable development from this car, nobody other than a blind man could deny the source of inspiration.

As we have seen in the previous chapter, it was necessary if the market for the Mark III Sunbeam was to be maintained that a new car embodying a combined body-chassis construction should be offered. Rootes' engineers were in fact among the pioneers of this method of construction in this country and the new Rapier announced at the 1955 Show was not only good-looking but soundly engineered with an eye to competition success. Incidentally, the car was smaller than the Mark III saloon, but it had a good deal more room inside, as well as weighing six hundredweight less. Just as its body harked back to the Minx Californian, so its engine was a development of the $76 \cdot 2 \times 76 \cdot 2$ mm, 1,390 cc, four-cylinder ohv engine introduced for the Minx in the previous year. The compression ratio was raised to 8 : 1 and produced 62 bhp at 5,000 rpm, giving a top speed of about

90 mph. A Laycock overdrive was offered as an optional extra, as was a rev counter, and indeed the whole set-up of the car from the driver's point of view was clearly one which rallyists would enjoy. The four-speed gearbox was borrowed from the Humber Hawk and as overdrive was available on top and third it became in effect a six-speed gearbox, even though much of the benefit was lost because two of the ratios were more or less identical. Conventional king pins were eliminated from the steering, the stub-axle carriers turning in the top suspension ball joints, while short pivot pins and trunnions were used to support the bottom end. The Burman steering had reverted to worm and nut operation and the centre portion of the three-piece track rod performed a perpetually phenomenal avoidance round the top of the clutch housing. An anti-roll bar was fitted to the front and it was found possible to dispense with the Panhard rod at the rear since the frame structure was now so rigid. In common with most other cars of this period, hydraulic operation was used for both clutch and brake and it is perhaps a permissibly amusing aside to observe that this system had also been used in the Sunbeam Silver Bullet way back in 1930.

Some further account of the differences between the engine first put into the Rapier and the standard Hillman Minx may be of interest to readers. In fact, few modifications were carried out; the compression ratio was increased from 7 : 1 to 8 : 1, a Stromberg $1\frac{1}{32}$-inch choke DIF36 carburettor fitted in place of a Zenith and the manifolding modified. The Minx camshaft and valves were retained, giving a valve timing of inlet opens 11° BTDC, inlet closes 55° ABDC, exhaust opens 53° BBDC and exhaust closes 13° ATDC. The Humber Hawk gearbox was not in itself modified but was fitted on one side so as to bring the selector mechanism to the top of the box (which was to come in handy when the competition department wanted to fit a short, stiff gear lever). The result of these modifications was to increase the output of the 1·4 Minx engine from 43 bhp at 4,400 rpm to 57·5 bhp (or, as some say, 62) at 5,000 rpm, the BMEP being 130 lbs per square inch at 3,000 rpm and the torque 878 lbs/ins at 3,000 rpm—these figures in fact refer to an engine on the test bed with the exhaust system in place, but without the gearbox.

Initial testing began something like two years before the model appeared on the market and much of it was carried out at the Motor Industry Research Association's testing ground, although cars were sent off just before the announcement through Spain, Switzerland and Italy, and Garrad, who was at that time not only competition manager but sales manager for Sunbeam Talbot,

had been to Sweden to demonstrate the car to some journalists
to see what he could find out for himself.

The car made its competition début in the Mille Miglia of
June 1956. Two cars were entered, which finished second and
third in the 1,600 cc special touring class. They were driven by
Peter Harper and Sheila van Damm, who managed the 1,000 miles
in fifteen hours, four minutes, thirty-seven seconds, and by
Wisnewski and Bosmiller, who followed close behind them in
fifteen hours, twenty-two minutes, one second. In fact, a number
of British production cars had competed and nearly all had done
well. Some of them at least had been more or less out-and-out
sports cars and the Rapier in holding its own in these circumstances certainly had nothing to be ashamed of. Four cars were
entered in the Tulip Rally and four cars finished, one of them—
a private entry in the hands of John Melvin—being first in the
1,300 to 1,600 cc class.

Later on that year another private owner, 'Doc' Deane, had
finished first in the Normal Series Production class of the Alpine
Rally, although three of the cars in this event came to disaster.
Looking back, it is fairly clear that the handling characteristics
of the first Rapiers still left a good deal to be desired, one contemporary road test stating, 'while the car will get round corners
quickly, the driver is left in some doubt as to his security if he
drives over the limits of adhesion. The steering is accurate, yet at
the same time it lacks feel, and the suspension permits more roll
—together with a feeling of flexibility—than is desirable in a car
of the Rapier's performance.' Indeed, everybody complained of
the lack of 'feel' between the steering wheel and the road and while
it is probably true that the regular team drivers got used to this,
strenuous efforts were made to improve it and there is no doubt
that the present Rapier shows how successful these efforts were.

In September 1956 a slightly modified engine known as the
R67 was announced, which, while remaining at the original
capacity of 1,390 cc, was able to provide by the introduction of
twin carburettors 67·5 bhp at 5,000 rpm instead of the 62 bhp,
previously available. The observant reader will note that the 1957
Monte Carlo Rally is missing from the list of successes which
appears in Appendix I, but no one can win all the time and,
indeed, it was a thin year throughout for the team, whose only
win in a rally which counted for the championship was a class
victory in the Tulip by Jimmy Ray and Ian Hall.

However, with the return of the Mille Miglia the Rapier was
able to repeat its previous year's performance of coming second
in that difficult and strenuous event. A class win in the Tulip

Peter Harper, Alpine Rally 1956. Tyres being marked with hot irons to make sure that the cars finish with the same tyres as they started with. This is the first event in which competitors had to keep the same tyres from start to finish

Rally is about all we have to record before coming to the beginning of 1958, when things began looking up with a vengeance.

The 1958 Monte Carlo was a rather undistinguished Rally dominated by the Renault contingent and by the bad weather. It was tough, but curious since the choice of starting-point had a great effect on the results, and nothing could have been worse than Paris. In fact, 243 cars retired before the finish and one could say that every one of the fifty-nine which arrived had enjoyed some measure of success. One would like to think that the severe conditions were responsible for most of the retirements, but in fact a good deal of the trouble was mechanical. The BBC Humber was in a bad way by the time it reached Paris; Ivor Bueb's Rapier seized up and Merrick's car broke a dynamo bracket. The Independent Television Authority had come into being and, not to be

outdone by the BBC, also had a Humber in the Rally, but this
managed to suffer with its distributor and fan belt. Nevertheless,
on the good side the Sunbeam Rapier, driven by Peter Harper,
won the award for the highest-placed British car and indeed was
one of the only nine cars out of the fifty-nine survivors to finish the
road section with a clean sheet. An interesting sidelight on this
performance was that the works cars were now fitted with a non-
standard floor-mounted gear-change, which will serve admirably
as a lever into the next chapter.

chapter 5 **The Sharpened Edge**

On 6 February 1958 Rootes announced the Series II Rapier. The bore of the engine was increased to give over-square dimensions of 79 × 76·2 mm, with compression ratio raised from 8 : 1 to 8·5 : 1. The valve diameter was increased by 1/16th of an inch on both inlet and exhaust and the porting was improved. As if to give credit where credit was due, the engine was referred to as the new Rallymaster and gave 73 bhp gross, or if you prefer it, 68 bhp net, at 5,200 rpm. Twin Zenith carburettors were fitted.

Other modifications included twin silencers, raised gear ratios, a central remote-control gear lever (directly inherited from the competition department), and the brake lining area increased by 25·5 per cent, by making the front brake drums ten inches in diameter in place of the previous nine inches. The steering gear was revised and stiffer front suspension fitted. The styling was improved, both inside and out, and the new Sunbeam type grille was fitted on to the radiator, despite the fact that the car was evidently designed to have a single slit; and, presumably to give the crew something to hold on to when they were walking round the car on ice, fins in the shape of a handrail decorated the rear half of the car. The new arrangements with the gear lever were an immediate success, William Boddy writing in *Motor Sport*: 'The new gear-change is a vast improvement and in keeping with the character of the Sunbeam. The lever is placed exactly right and has a man-sized flat knob, which on one occasion came off in our hand. The gear-changes go through as rapidly as the driver desires and delightfully smoothly. . . .'

The maximum speed was in the neighbourhood of 90 mph, and 80 mph was readily attainable on any reasonable straight. At 4,500 rpm in top or 3,448 in overdrive the car was doing round

about 70 mph. Even at 80 mph in overdrive top the engine speed
was under 4,000 rpm. Driven really hard, about 28 mpg was
possible, and one does not have to give much thought to the situation to realize that here was a car born out of competition developments with an eye to the main chance in foreign rallies in the
future.

Turning back to the world of competition, we come to the
RAC Rally in 1958, which the new Series II Rapier succeeded in
winning outright in the hands of Harper and Deane. The Rally,
starting from either Hastings or Blackpool, consisted mostly of a
series of special tests interspersed with road sections. The weather
was practically Arctic and after climbing Prescott Hill there was
a manoeuvring test at Chateau Impney and some highly exciting
dicing on ice over the War Department ranges at Epynt. After this
there were tests or racing at Lydstep, Oulton Park, Aintree,
Blackpool, Tow Top, Ulpha, Charterhall, Otterburn, Croft,
Sherburn-in-Elmet, Chapel-en-le-Frith, Snetterton, Mallory,
Silverstone, Brands and Hastings, in all 1,800 miles and one might
say the Tour de France in embryo. So on the whole the car got off
to a good start. Harper and Deane were actually driving VRW269,
a car which had a tremendously long and successful career in the
Rootes team, not only in rallies but eventually in racing. Their
win was all the more creditable since they had had to stop when
Nancy Mitchell had crashed in the wilds of Northumberland for
the doctor to administer medical aid. A team prize was secured in
the Tulip Rally of that year, but unfortunately the event was
blighted by the death of one of the Mercedes drivers during the
special test at Zandvoort. The conditions had been very severe
throughout the Rally and in point of fact, although the team
prize went to Sunbeam, none of the cars was in the first nine of the
general results. During the same year an outright win was secured
at a rally in Uganda and in the Scottish Rally the team achieved
first and third places for modified touring cars in their group.

It was, however, in the Alpine Rally (it is extraordinary how
the 'Monte' and the Alpine together seem from time immemorial
to have been the Sunbeam-Talbot hunting grounds) that the
year's best effort was seen. The team achieved first, second, third,
fourth and fifth places in their class, a Coupe des Alpes and a
third place in the Coupe des Dames. The Rally was very tough
that year, starting from Marseilles on the Monday afternoon of
7 July, going up into the French Alps, over the Allos, Izoard and
Vars to the French/Italian frontier on the Mont Genèvre about
midnight. On to Monza Autodrome by dawn for a special test,
after which the competitors went on to Brescia where the first

Alpine Rally 1959: one of the team cars being tested at Scrutineering to see that the boot lid is made of steel

stage ended and the cars were locked away for the night. At four o'clock the next morning they set off again for the Dolomites over the really tough gravelled pass of the Vivione, going north-eastwards as far as Bolzano and Merano. They turned back over the Stelvio and Gavia, back across the Vivione and into Milan as darkness fell. In the night they crossed the Grand St. Bernard back into France for the end of the second stage at Megève. On Friday morning after a rest they tramped up and down and around the passes in the Chambéry/Grenoble area, arriving at Gap just before darkness fell. There was a short break and then during the night the Glandon, Telegraphe, Galibier, Lautaret, Izoard, Vars, etc., going southwards over the Cayolle and then back north again over the Allos. Back to Mont Ventoux and finally down to Marseilles where they arrived on Saturday afternoon, still having before them a five-lap race in the local park. Anyone who wins a prize in an event like this has really done a magnificent job.

As usual, Peter Harper emerged near the top of the lists, this time in company with Peter Jopp. They succeeded in winning their class prize and finished sixth overall. There is no doubt that by this time the Rootes competition department had really got to grips with the regulations and those little bits of knowledge which make all the difference to the running of the team in the event, and this, coupled with very careful preparation of the cars which provided useful improvements in power output, was beginning to pay dividends. There seemed every reason to suppose that 1959 would be a bumper year for the marque—and indeed it was.

Beginning as usual with the Monte Carlo Rally, Adams and McMillen finished fifth overall, being the best British entry, Ivor Bueb and Scott being sixteenth in the same event, while Gregor, Grant and McCaldin were near the end of the list but were nevertheless among the finishers.

In true Sunbeam Talbot fashion, we now pass on to the Alpine which was run, if anything, over even rougher roads than the

Alpine Rally 1958: Peter Harper's Rapier at speed during the final test of the rally on Parc Borely, Marseilles

Alpine Rally 1958: Tommy Sopwith in a Rapier. This is the heartbreak of rallying; only 4/5 of a second separated him from a penalty-free run and a coveted Coupe des Alpes

previous year, and it is more than usually creditable that Paddy Hopkirk and Jack Scott finished third overall, having to give pride of place only to two high-performance GT cars. Peter Jopp and Les Leston were sixth. Not the least interesting thing about this event was a startling demonstration by Ronnie Adams of exactly how strongly constructed the Sunbeam Rapier is. He had a really beastly accident late on in the Rally when he had to swerve into a concrete post to avoid a large lorry. The post tore away the offside body more or less completely, but Adams, despite having had his head in very sharp contact with the windscreen, tied the door up with a bit of rope and drove the car back to Cannes, where it was quite a sensation, along with the new Sunbeam Alpine which Norman Garrad introduced at a party when the event was over.

The Liège–Rome–Liège was next on the list and was as tough as usual. In fact, of the ninety-seven starters only fourteen got to the finish at all; one of them, a Sunbeam Rapier driven by Jimmy

Ray and Mike Cotton, finished eleventh overall and won its class. Just before the London Motor Show that year the new Series III was announced and yet another piece of this fascinating jigsaw on the development of one of Britain's most successful competition cars was about to be put into place.

As is usual in a development of this kind, there were no very startling changes and the man in the street or on the stand at the Show may not have recognized very quickly in which direction the improvements lay. Apart from improved performance from the engine, the most interesting innovation was the addition of disc brakes for the front wheels. Returning to the engine, this unit had now been given an aluminium cylinder head and the power output had been increased by 5 bhp to the figure of 78 bhp at 5,400 rpm. The compression ratio with the new aluminium head was raised to 9·2 : 1. The design of the valves was also somewhat modified by a new arrangement of inlet and exhaust porting, while new twin carburettors and a water-heated inlet manifold certainly made the engine more lively. The gear ratios were again revised, bringing both second and third gears close to top, and the angle of gear lever movement was reduced to provide shorter travel and quicker operation. It only takes half an eye to see the influence of competition motoring in these modifications. To accommodate the new disc brakes the front track was widened, which also had the effect of further improving the road-holding and stability.

The bodywork as usual underwent various changes; a larger windscreen giving a 20 per cent increase in forward vision was incorporated and the quality of the interior trim improved. The polished walnut facia was now surmounted with a padded safety roll.

Meanwhile the team used the old models for the RAC Rally, now moved to its new date. This event proved something of a disaster for the Rootes team; Malkin and Robson in a privately entered Series II finished fifth overall and were second in their class, but the bulk of the works entry were penalized for being late at the Braemar control after scenes of utter chaos caused by the blockage of a mountain road in the Scottish Highlands.

As soon as this event was over, the personnel returned to Ryton-on-Dunsmore for a period of frenzied activity in the preparation of the new Series III cars for a competition life. Garrad's wisdom in appreciating the difficulties of regulations, both for individual events and on an international basis, was shown by the policy of offering many parts from the new Sunbeam Alpine as optional equipment on the Series III Rapier, thus allowing a much improved car to pass the F.I.A. homologation. The cars were registered YWK1, 2, 3, 4 and 5 and were eventually to become almost as famous as Roesch's original Talbots, GO51, 52 and 53.

To begin the new season in the accustomed manner Peter Harper, accompanied by Raymond Baxter of the BBC in YWK5, finished fourth in the Monte Carlo Rally and put up the best performance by a British entry. Not only was Harper really able to get in among the Germans, but his performance must be regarded as doubly creditable since Raymond Baxter became ill during the mountain circuit and Harper had to drive most of it unaided by his navigator and with a strong suspicion that some of the navigational instruments were more than slightly inaccurate.

Harper was joined by Procter for the Acropolis Rally and the two Peters began developing a very successful partnership, being fourth overall in Greece and winning their class the following month in the Alpine. The RAC Rally once more, as in the previous year, saw Rapier fortunes at a low ebb, crashes eliminating two of the entries.

However, the overall picture of 1960 as a Sunbeam year was far from bad, for the marque recorded class wins in the Monte Carlo, the Circuit of Ireland, the Acropolis and the Alpine, and 1960 also saw the works Sunbeams appearing regularly in production car racing for the first time. After class wins at Silverstone and Brands Hatch, the year was brought to a successful conclusion by a class win on a foreign circuit when a Sunbeam Rapier beat off fairly strong foreign competition in the International Compact Car Race at Riverside, California.

The new year, 1961, begins, as far as our story is concerned, on 21 January with another Monte Carlo Rally. No fewer than twenty-one of the 110 British entries were driving Rootes Group cars. Six Rapiers competing as two separate teams represented the works entry, driven by Harper, Hopkirk, Ray, Jopp, Mary Handley Page and Gregor Grant; the latter, partnered by Michael Parkes—now of Ferrari but then of the Rootes Group—started from Warsaw. When the results came to be published, it was found that for the fourth successive year a Sunbeam Rapier was the highest placed British car. The superb drive by Harper in the final Classification Test round the Grand Prix Circuit with a best lap of 2 minutes 15·1 seconds (beating many more powerful Continental cars) secured for him a class win. For the second year in succession Sweden's Rune Backlund and Nils Falk won the 1,300–2,000 cc class for Grand Touring cars in their Sunbeam Alpine.

*The start in Mexico when the Rodriguez brothers took 1st and 2nd place
in the up to 1600 cc class for production cars. They defeated by a clear
lap a field of sixteen makes, including French, German, Italian, Japanese
and other British entries*

*Sebring 1961: Vince Tamburo who had previously won the national
championship in the G Production Cars*

While all this was going on, two Sunbeam Rapiers, brilliantly
conducted by the young Rodriguez brothers, gained a spectacular
international victory in Mexico's major race meeting. The race
was in fact a private duel between Pedro and Ricardo, who finally
finished only fifteen seconds apart, Ricardo, the winner, turning
in the fastest lap at 69·8 mph (112·5 kph).

The racing scene was continued with the entry of four Sunbeam
Alpines (two from the works), one entered by Jack Brabham and
one private entry at Sebring on 25 March. However, the racing
situation here was soon to be eclipsed by the announcement of
another Rapier class win, this time in the notorious East African
Safari. Of the seventy-seven competitors who started, only thirty-
eight finished and a Rapier, driven by J. P. Valumbia, a garage
proprietor from Morogoro in Tanganyika, with one I. M. Bakhsh
as his co-driver, won Class C without trouble. No prizes were won
by Dr Lee Talbot and Mohamed Iqbal, who nevertheless put up a
good show in a Super Snipe by finishing fourth overall. A few

*East African Safari Rally, 1962: Dr Lee Talbot, US Wild Life research
scientist, in a Super Snipe shortly after the start from Nairobi*

days later a Sunbeam Alpine won the 1,001–3,000 cc class in the
Sports and Production Car Race at Pietermaritzburg, and, back
on his home ground if not actually ours, Paddy Hopkirk achieved
an outright win in the Circuit of Ireland.

On 20 April this year the Series IIIA Sunbeam Rapier was
introduced with the engine increased to 1,592 cc (because of the
1,600 cc Rally Class), which considerably improved the performance. The engine was in fact the same as that already installed
in the Sunbeam Alpine.

The engine retained its aluminium cylinder head and twin
carburettors, but had the compression ratio increased to 9·1 : 1,
giving a power output of 80·25 bhp at 5,100 rpm, compared with
the 78 bhp at 5,400 rpm of the 1,494 cc unit. Maximum torque
was also increased from 84 lb/ft at 3,500 rpm to 88·2 lb/ft at 3,900
rpm. To match this increased power a stiffer crankshaft was fitted
together with larger diameter connecting rod bearings with
modified connecting rods and gudgeon pins.

No great kudos was achieved in the Tulip, but the widespread
use of Sunbeam Rapiers by private entries must be regarded as an

*Robert Topman, the South African racing driver, at speed at the
Roy Hesketh circuit*

encouraging feature from a sales point of view. British, Dutch and Swiss crews drove Rapiers in the Rootes-entered team, while two private owners from Denmark, Nielsen and Jensen, who had been the highest placed Danish crew in the Monte Carlo, also drove a Rapier.

The name of Hillman now appears in the lists, winning the 1,500 cc class in the South African Tour of Natal, a fact which apparently encouraged Rootes (Canada) Ltd to enter three Hillman Minx saloons in the Trans-Canada Rally—no one can say they weren't trying!

Back home at Silverstone during the International Trophy meeting on 6 May, Harper put in a lap at 83·2 mph in a Rapier to shatter the lap record for the class, which he had himself established the previous October. Meanwhile, as the sun got up in the

The winning Alpine is flagged across the finishing line at Le Mans where
it won the Thermal Efficiency Award

sky, a determined assault was made in the Acropolis Rally when three Rapiers won the Team Prize. Of the eighty-three competing cars, Rapiers driven by Harper/Procter, Ballisat/Jopp, and Ray/Hall took fifth, sixth and ninth places in the General Classification.

Back home, John Melvin, a Glasgow Rootes dealer, and his wife Ann won the Scottish Rally outright. The 1,000-mile event incorporated eight special stages and might be regarded as something of a forerunner of the present British Rally. At Le Mans Sunbeams made a triumphal return when Harper and Procter won the Index of Thermal Efficiency at an average speed of 91 mph (146 kph), covering 2,194 miles (3,511 kilometres) without any untoward stop. It was incidental, but nevertheless rewarding, to find Harper the first to cross the finishing line after the chequered flag fell at 4 p.m. The Alpine was in fact the first works-entered Sunbeam since 1925, when J. Chassagne and S. C. H. Davies drove a 3-litre car into second place at 55·9 mph. When the race was over, Harper said that the car had given no trouble either to himself or his co-driver, Peter Procter, and was in fact going as well on the last lap as at any stage of the race.

For the Alpine which followed, three Rapiers and one Alpine were entered with Harper and Procter in one, Hopkirk and Scott in another, and a new crew of Ballisat and 'Tiny' Lewis in a third car. The Alpine was driven by Mary Handley Page and Mrs Pauline Mayman.

For reasons known only to God and Garrad, and probably largely due to the latter's experience, the Alpine seems always to be the event in which the Sunbeam Talbot dynasty has achieved its greatest success, and this year was no exception. Only twenty-five of the sixty-four starters reached the finish after four days and nights of leaping round the roof-top of Europe, and the team of Harper, Hopkirk and Ballisat drove victoriously into Cannes at the end of the event to win the award for the best team irrespective of size, class or nationality, and to notch up their third win on the cup presented to the best foreign team, so making it Sunbeam property. They also took the Gatsonides Cup for the team making the best times in the special tests. Hopkirk came third in the Rally overall and won the 1,300 to 1,600 cc class. This was in fact the seventh time since the war that Sunbeams won their class in this gruelling event and spirits were running particularly high this year since it was also the tenth major award to be won by the marque in rallies and races during the previous six months.

Cuff-Miller of Littlehampton won his class in the Production Touring Car Race of the British Empire Trophy Meeting in July, and on the other side of the Atlantic Jack Brabham and Stirling Moss won their class and took third place overall in the three hours' endurance race for sports cars at Riverside, California. For the first time Sunbeams entered the Tour de France and 'Tiny' Lewis again appeared in the team, this time as co-driver to Paddy Hopkirk.

Rapiers won the Team Prize in the RAC Rally which, as usual, seemed to play havoc with the cars, Peter Procter having had a puncture on one of the special sections in Wales, stopped to change a wheel, started again and got another puncture! On this occasion he felt he had no time to muck about changing wheels, so drove on at full bore for nearly twenty miles. It did not take long for the rubber to wear away but, undaunted, he continued on a very buckled rim, managed to finish the section and so ensured that Sunbeams got the Team Prize. But even this stout effort was somewhat overshadowed by a remarkable performance by Raymond Baxter of the BBC, who, with Leonard Miller, drove a very 'executive' Super Snipe into first place for the over 1,600 cc class in Series Production cars. So much for 1961.

This catalogue of success becomes almost a bore when committed to paper, but it remains fascinating when the effort required for its achievement is considered, the whole thing having been achieved on six Rapiers and three Alpines, which shuttled back

'Tiny' Lewis and Keith Ballisat in the 1961 Alpine

Alpine Rally 1961: the comprehensively-equipped facia of one of the Sunbeam Rapier cars. The driver's comfort is a necessity, not a luxury

and forth from the extremities of Europe to the brightly-lit recesses of the competition department at Ryton-on-Dunsmore where more oil was burnt in midnight lamps than was ever consumed by the engines. The mechanical effort is one thing, but when one considers the paperwork involved in making the entries alone, leaving aside all consideration of the number of cross-Channel air tickets and boat tickets that need to be acquired and the amount of bribery and corruption which needs to be indulged in to get an unexpected casualty back from France in mid-summer and a replacement out to somewhere else on the same weekend as Mr and Mrs Smith have decided to take their holiday, it all seems an almost unbearable effort. There were many times in the year when the staff of the competition department felt that they could not see the cars for paper.

Once more the calendar had turned the full circle and the Monte Carlo Rally was again to prove a happy hunting ground. The Rapiers won both the major team awards, won their class for the third successive year and took five of the first seventeen places in the Rally, despite the fact that Hopkirk was fighting a very severe bout of flu throughout the two thousand miles. It is not often that a manufacturer finishes a Rally to produce such a list of awards as this:

AWARD	CLASS	DRIVERS
Charles Faroux Trophy	Manufacturers' Team Prize	P. Hopkirk P. Procter P. Harper
Challenge Equipe	Highest placed three cars of the same make	P. Hopkirk P. Procter P. Harper
Riviera Cup	Winner 1,300–1,600 cc class	P. Hopkirk
Royal Automobile Club Trophy	Best performance in a British car	P. Hopkirk
British Automobile Racing Club Cup	Best performance by member	P. Procter
British Trials and Rally Drivers' Association Trophy	Best performance by member	P. Harper
Challenge Antony Noghes	Best performance by competitor who has taken part in at least ten Monte Carlo Rallies	P. Harper
Autosport Trophy	Best performance in a privately owned British car	Dr J. T. Spare
First Prize	Speed and manoeuvrability trials	P. Hopkirk

Harking back to the difficulties of preparing cars, we come to one of the brightest anecdotes in the history of the competition department. At the conclusion of the Monte Carlo, Maxence Balas, the Rootes Group dealer in Grenoble, talked Garrad into promising him a car for the French Snow and Ice Rally which began within seven days of the car's arrival in Monte. History does not relate whether this arrangement was actually concluded in the bar of the Hotel Metropole or elsewhere, but there was certainly no time to get a properly prepared works car and in fact the enthusiastic Monsieur Balas simply drove away from Monte Carlo in the car which Peter Harper had just used to win his class. Back at the garage in Grenoble there was only time to change the oil and to grease it before he set off, but although the Rapier had just covered 2,500 miles in the previous week in the course of the Monte Carlo Rally, and although Balas had never driven a right-hand car in a competition before, he won the 1,100–1,600 cc class and came second in the general touring classification, starting from Chambéry on a thirteen-hour Rally which was snow and ice all the way. The Rapier was one of only three cars to finish the road section unpenalized and Balas, with his co-driver, Gérard Chevron, had a wonderful trip, announcing at the end—no doubt for the benefit of the Press but with perfect truth: 'The car is as good now as when it set out at the Monte Carlo Rally. I am sure it could do it all again.'

Come April, Eugene Bosman in South Africa improved on his last year's effort by winning the Tour of Natal outright in a Hillman Minx. Three Minxes and three Super Snipes were entered for the Safari and Hillman Minx saloons won first and second places in the 1,300–1,600 cc class, all three Minxes finishing the event, in spite of torrential rain which turned hundreds of miles of the route into deep, almost impenetrable, mud, so that fewer than half of the 104 starters succeeded in arriving at the finish in Nairobi.

The Minx also won its class in the Seven-Day Trans-Canada Rally held from Montreal to Vancouver, while with what can now be described as almost metronomic regularity Hopkirk, driving a Rapier, won the Circuit of Ireland.

Some idea of the effort which Rootes were at this time putting into their competition work can be gleaned from a modest statement issued on 19 April:

The Rootes Group is about to enter into the most intensive period of direct participation in motor sport in its history.

During the next three months the Group—firm believers in the value of motoring events as a tough but effective means of improving its products—will compete in eight international events in Britain and abroad.

The programme includes production car races, three international rallies and, of course, the classic Le Mans 24-hour endurance race for sports cars. This crowded schedule begins at Easter, when Rootes factory drivers will be involved in no less than three different international events.

Peter Harper will be driving a Rapier in the production car race at Goodwood on Easter Monday; his team-mate, Paddy Hopkirk, will be at the wheel of another Rapier in the Circuit of Ireland Rally; and six cars (three Humber Super Snipes and three Hillman Minx De Luxe Saloons) will be competing in the gruelling four-day East African Safari Rally.

The rest of the Rootes short-term competition programme includes the production car race at Aintree on April 28th; the production car race at Silverstone on May 12th; the International Acropolis Rally in Greece, beginning May 27th; the Le Mans 24-hour race on June 23rd/24th and the production car race at the British Grand Prix Meeting at Aintree in July.

Rootes cars will be entered in other events later in the year, including the Tour de France, that 'rally of the races'. 'We consider this full competitions programme to be an extension of our testing work,' said a Rootes Group spokesman. 'Motor sporting events provide a gruelling test of both car and driver and play an invaluable part in improving the product.'

As a competition manager, Garrad always had a great belief in running a good all-woman crew, not only for the chances of the Coupes des Dames prizes, but also because they clearly provide a good deal of publicity. Many serious enthusiasts tend to take a 'dim view' of the publicity aspect of competition motoring, but it is a hard if somewhat unpalatable truth that one of the fundamental reasons why manufacturers enter competitions at all is for the effect of the publicity. Few firms can have made more of the engineering possibilities than the Rootes Organisation, but the fact remains that rallying for the sake of engineering alone would hardly be a proposition.

For some eighteen months past the Organisation had not had a girls' crew and ears pricked up, therefore, when with the announcement that the usual team was to be entered for the Acropolis Rally, the name of Rosemary Smith turned up as a contender. At the time she joined the Rootes team Rosemary Smith was twenty-four and had already been rallying seriously for two years, having won the Ladies' Award in the Circuit of Ireland twice, finished third in the Ladies' Class in the 1961 RAC, and collected a cupboardful of pots for her efforts in various other trials, hill climbs, races and autocross events. She was by profession the proprietor of a small couture business in Dublin and a designer-consultant to a large Dublin fashion house, and she joined the team to follow in the wheel tracks of Sheila van Damm and Mary Handley Page.

For the Acropolis, apart from the works team, there was a Rapier entered by Nicky Filinis, the Rootes Group dealer in Athens.

When it came to the event, Filinis won his class and Rosemary

Mary Handley Page in a 1960 Alpine

Smith made a very successful début by finishing immediately behind him. Back on the other side of the world, a Hillman Super Minx got an outright win in the Columbian Canyon Rally, a tough event held in the pine-clad mountains and ravines of British Columbia.

Again on the racing circuits, Sunbeam Rapiers finished first, second and third in the Improved Touring Car Race of the Grand Prix de Spa, Lucien Bianchi averaging 95·9 mph (154·35 kph) on the Spa–Francorchamps Circuit—a success which followed within only eight days of the Silverstone event in which Rapiers, as usual, occupied the first four places in their class.

Three Alpines were entered for Le Mans and Rosemary Smith was nominated as the reserve driver, a nomination which was not accepted by the organisers of the race but was accepted by the Press wholeheartedly to the tune of several hundred single-column inches.

Andrew Cowan and David Thompson won the Scottish Rally outright, repeating Procter's performance with a flat tyre, only this time going on for so long that they wore the wheel down to the brake drum, completing the special section in question within sixteen seconds of the fastest time of any competitor. Which leads a historian looking back from this distance to the conclusion that most of the other competitors cannot have been going very fast!

A full team of three Rapiers was entered for the Tour de France, driven by Harper/Procter, Ballisat/Lewis and, taking part in the event for the first time, Rosemary Smith and Rosemary Seers. Also competing was a French-entered Sunbeam Alpine driven by Nail and Français, Rootes Group dealers from La Rochelle. The event started from Rouen on 15 September and did not finish at Rheims until 23 September. In the eight-and-a-half days of motoring the Tour embraced seven circuit races (one of two hours' duration) and seven high-speed hill climb events, together with fast sections on normal roads totalling 5,000 kms (comfortably over 3,000 miles). Once more things turned out well, the team winning first, second and third places in their class. But the real triumph was for twenty-four-year-old Rosemary Smith, who won not only the Ladies' Prize, but the Special Ladies' Handicap Award, thus proving herself and absolutely justifying Garrad's choice. It was also something of a smack in the eye for the French authorities who had refused to accept her as reserve driver in the Sunbeam team at Le Mans on the grounds that a woman could not match men in this high-speed event. The irony of the situation is perhaps best appreciated when one realizes that among the circuits included in the Tour de France was Le Mans!

Brabham and McLaren re-united under the Rootes Group banner at Riverside, California, in the autumn to head a six-car team of Sunbeam Alpines which was entered for the three-hour Endurance Race, but the events in the autumn were perhaps overshadowed by a jubilee celebration by the Rootes Organisation at the Paris Motor Show.

Fifty years of major achievement in international motor sport was symbolized at the Paris Show in 1962 by two historic Sunbeam racing cars of 1912 and 1924 in the vintage sports car section and by the modern Sunbeam Alpines and Rapiers on the Rootes Group's stand.

The 1912 3-litre model, with its blunt nose and waspish tail, gave Sunbeam their first major international success when a team of three of the cars finished first, second and third in the Coupe de L'Auto at Dieppe.

It was a classic victory for the British company, which had started manufacturing cars in 1899 and was beginning to build an international reputation under the inspiration of its French-born chief engineer and designer, Louis Coatalen.

More than forty cars had entered for the race which was run

jointly with the French Grand Prix—and in addition to their clean sweep in the Coupe de L'Auto Sunbeams also took third, fourth and fifth places in the Grand Prix itself. They were beaten only by two cars of respectively two-and-a-half and five times their engine capacity which achieved average speeds of only 3 mph (4·8 kph) greater.

The winning Sunbeam, driven by Victor Rigal, covered 956 miles (1,538 km) in the race at an average speed of over 65 mph (104 kph)—and this exhibition of speed and reliability by these comparatively small four-cylinder cars signalled the end of the era of monster-engined models on European circuits and started a new trend in racing car design. In the same year the Coupe de L'Auto Sunbeam captured a number of world records at Brooklands at speeds up to 86 mph (138 kph).

In the years that followed Coatalen utilized his genius for engine design in many other directions. Sunbeam-Coatalen engines powered a range of British and French aircraft during the 1914–18 war; they powered the R.34 airship which made the first successful flights from Britain to the USA and back; they powered a range of successful marine craft including the speed-boat which won the 1920 Championship of the Sea at Monaco.

Meanwhile, a series of motor racing successes reached a climax when 2-litre Sunbeams took first, second and fourth places in the 1923 French Grand Prix at Tours—and on the same day Coatalen was nominated Chevalier of the Legion of Honour for his war-time services to aviation.

The 1924 2-litre Sunbeam was developed from these victorious cars and was the first British supercharged racing car. In this model Coatalen pioneered a new technique of supercharging which was subsequently adopted by all other major European manufacturers.

These cars made their first appearance in the 1924 French Grand Prix but after leading the race and establishing the fastest lap were forced to retire with faulty magnetos. In the same year, however, Sir Henry Segrave drove one of these cars to victory in the Spanish Grand Prix at an average speed of 63·5 mph (102 kph).

Subsequently one of these cars was purchased by Kaye Don who named it 'The Cub' and, partnered by Captain G. E. T. Eyston, established a number of long distance world records at speeds of up to 126 mph (203 kph).

Meanwhile, the Sunbeam company had switched its attention from the race track to the world land speed record and in March, 1927, Sir Henry Segrave in a specially built 1,000 horse-power

Sunbeam pushed the record from 170 mph (273 kph) to 203 mph (326 kph) at Daytona Beach in Florida.

Economic pressures forced Sunbeams' retirement from racing in the early 1930s but after the Company had been reorganised and incorporated into the Rootes Group, Lord Rootes, who had raced motor cycles himself as a young man, determined to maintain Sunbeams' sporting reputation in the world's toughest motor rallies.

In the post-war years Sunbeams have consistently proved themselves among Europe's most successful rally cars and have won major honours in every event in the international rally calendar.

In the Monte Carlo Rally alone, Sunbeams have scored an outright victory and won the manufacturers' team prize four times—and for brilliance and consistency, their performance in 1962, when five Rapiers were among the first eleven cars in the general classification, ranked with the epic achievements of the past.

During recent years, Sunbeams have also successfully returned to the race track in production car events and Alpines have figured among the finishers in the last two Le Mans 24-hour races, winning the Index of Thermal Efficiency Award in the 1961 event. In 1962 Sunbeam Rapiers took first and second places in their class in the saloon car championship organised by the British Racing and Sports Car Club.

When he entered the 3-litre cars for the 1912 Coupe de L'Auto Louis Coatalen, who died in 1962 in Paris, declared: 'If we go in for this race we must regard it not as a speculation to win but as the most effective means of learning how still further to improve our standard model against the next manufacturing season.'

This policy is as alive in the Rootes Group today as it was when Sunbeams first donned British racing green.

Sunbeam 3-litre Coupe de L'Auto. This car was bought by Lord Montagu and restored to its original condition and is normally on display at the Montagu Motor Museum at Beaulieu in Hampshire.

Engine: 4-cylinder sv	Gearbox: 4-speed	Brakes:
		Foot on transmission
		Hand on rear wheels
Bore and Stroke:	Transmission: Shaft	
80 × 148 mm		Suspension: $\frac{1}{2}$-elliptic
Capacity: 2,996 cc	Body: 2-seat racing	

Brooklands Jubilee, June 1957. 2-litre supercharged 1924 Grand Prix Sunbeam known as The Cub. John Rowe at the wheel

Sunbeam 2-litre: 'The Cub'. This car has been restored to full racing trim by the Rootes Group.

Engine: 6-cylinder twin ohv	Gearbox: 4-speed	Brakes: Four-wheel
Bore and Stroke: 67 × 94 mm	Transmission: Shaft	Suspension: $\frac{1}{2}$-elliptic
Capacity: 1,988 cc	Body: 2-seat racing	
Ignition: HT magneto		

Class wins followed in the RAC Rally to bring 1962 to a satisfactory conclusion and there was the usual rush between the end of November and the beginning of January to prepare cars for the Monte, carry out the reconnaissance, and generally see what the next year could produce.

In point of fact, we have now got near the end of the story and the scene begins to change. Harper won his class again in the Monte and the customary awards were achieved in the Circuit of Ireland. Results during the year, of which details appear on pages 91-4, continue to be good and will probably go on in their present

vein between the time this book is written and the time it reaches
the public, but the wind of change has swept through the air
of rallying and the standard product, which is after all what the
Rapier represents, has had a harder and harder task to maintain
its position.

In an effort to beat the homologation situation, the Lotus
Cortina, the Mini-Cooper S, the three-carburettor 2-litre Triumph
Vitesse (which never went into production) have all been toyed
with in the system of development. The Saab, which Carlsson has
done so well in, has already been described by one of the sharper
wits as the Pukka Sahib, and the Volvo, which is now beginning
to figure in both European and American rallies, is in fact a
ten-year-old body shell, which is not even obtainable on the
British market, fitted with the latest engine.

Rootes are the last people to take such a situation lying down,
but it is fairly clear from the results of the 1963 rallies that the day
when a fairly standard four-seater production sports saloon could
be one of the dominating cars in international rallying is now past.

*Monte Carlo 1963: Procter's Rapier with flamethrower adjusted for
taking right-angle corners!*

We already know that there are plans for a V8 Sunbeam (with a huge Ford engine in it); the Imp is obviously capable of development in several different directions, and although the factory will make no comment the Press have already talked of a 90 mph two-seater. The astonishing performance put up by Harper in the big Super Snipe during the last RAC Rally makes one wonder what would happen if the engineering department should introduce, say, three downdraught Webers and a bunch of bananas. Drivers too need to become hairier than ever and, to use the current jargon, remain not only right slotted but switched on! Speculation is enjoyable and it is no part of this volume to spoil that pleasure, but it is clear from the present situation at Ryton-on-Dunsmore that just as Sunbeam did in the halcyon days and Talbot did in the 1930s, so today the Rootes competition department means business.

chapter 6 **For Example . . .**

It is obviously of interest to readers of this book to know precisely
how the Rootes works team functions, but as no two rallies are
ever the same it is not possible to make a generalized statement
which applies to every particular case.

The following notes are, therefore, made on the exact function
of the Rootes Organisation in one particular rally—the RAC
Rally, 1963. The event, as it turned out, was not a very successful
one for the Rootes Organisation, but this perhaps makes a detailed
examination of what went on more, rather than less, interesting
because when you are winning and everything is going all right
there is a good deal less to do. This, then, is a detailed account of
the functioning of one particular event, and it does not necessarily
apply to any other; but it is indicative of what goes on.

The RAC Rally of 1963 began at Blackpool at six o'clock on
the evening of Monday, 11 November. It followed some while
after the finish of the Tour de France, but its date coincided with
several international Motor Shows, and at the time when the
company in general and the competition department in particular
would like to have been free to devote themselves entirely to the
preparation of the cars for the RAC event there were in fact many
distractions in the air.

The new Rapier announced at the Motor Show was not ready
for homologation by the time the entries went in; and it therefore
became necessary to use the 'old' model. There were none of these
left at the factory and a search round the dealers also failed to
produce a new, that is to say unused, 'old' model. The cars that
had been used at the Tour de France had, therefore, to be prepared. This, of course, meant virtually rebuilding them. In addition it was decided to enter one of the ex-Le Mans Sunbeam

Norman Garrad (second on left) discussing details with members of his Monte Carlo Rally Sunbeam Rapier team Peter Harper, Peter Procter and Rosemary Seers, at 'briefing' at Ryton. Extreme left is Lewis Garrad

Alpines, which Rosemary Smith had used to win the Coupe des Dames in the Tour de France, for 'Tiny' Lewis to drive in the RAC, this to be in direct competition in the GT Class with the Lotus Cortina entered by Henry Taylor.

Since Raymond Baxter had had a class win in a previous RAC Rally with a Super Snipe, it was decided to let Peter Harper have one of these models in the big class. The object here was to spread the possible chances of success by the process of permutation. The Rapier team would consist of Peter Procter and David Mabbs, David Pollard and Tony Baines, and Rosemary Smith and Margaret Mackenzie, the last two, of course, also competing for the Ladies' Prize.

There were also nine other Rapiers in the hands of private owners and two Hillman Imps which, although privately entered, were being closely watched (and watched over) by the competition department, who obviously have eyes on the car's future and entertain some hope that in the fullness of time some equivalent to the Cooper-modified Minis and Mini S's may come their way.

There can be little doubt that such a wide spread over the classes was a good idea, but it brought with it a very considerable strain on the resources of the department. It is obviously much easier to prepare four Sunbeam Rapiers and let it go at that, but such a policy is not adventurous and while it may make for ease of operation in one particular event, it does very little for the future of the Organisation.

In point of fact, despite a great deal of overtime and high pressure work, the cars were not ready for the drivers until the very end of the week before the event started—a state of affairs which neither the drivers nor the management liked very much— but in the circumstances it was not possible to have the cars ready earlier, and everybody had to make the best of it.

On the organisation side, there had also been fairly recent changes (dating back in fact to just before the Tour de France). The department has now been set up under two heads, Norman Garrad remaining the competitions manager but now concentrating his responsibility on the preparation of the cars. John Rowe, now temporarily appointed team manager, thus became responsible for the appointment of the drivers and the running of the team in the field—although, of course, there was a strong overlap with Norman Garrad's side of the business and, in fact, Garrad himself was much in evidence throughout the event. To provide service, four separate servicing teams were set up, each of them in a separate car with one of the bosses, each carrying a wide range of spare parts and two mechanics from the department, who would know what to do with them (details of the constitution of the teams and the points at which they made service available are given at the end of the chapter).

The drivers, the cars and the support teams all made their way to the Imperial Hotel, Blackpool, on Sunday, 10 November, and it was not until late that evening that the road books for the Rally were given out. These, like those of the Tulip Rally, carry no map references because the foreign competitors are not used to maps with the grid system on them, but carry only the detailed direction signs, together with mileages. The British contingent in general and Rootes in particular were armed with one-inch ordnance maps of the area and nearly all the navigators spent the last night, when they should have been sleeping, transferring the route from the route book on to one-inch maps, the Rootes navigators having got together to do one section each and then copy from each other. Provided one was prepared to trust the other man's work this was at least a way of easing a burden. By Monday afternoon most of the panics were over save that with steady rain pouring and an obviously wet night ahead Peter Harper decided that he would like to have some Town and Country tyres for the back wheels at least of the Super Snipe. He had some fairly genuine misgivings about getting it up some of the hills in the special sections of the Lake District. Frantic telephoning all round the countryside at four o'clock on Monday afternoon failed to produce a suitable set of tyres any nearer than Birmingham and Dunlop's own service van had no possibility of getting hold of these until they got to Carlisle after the first two special sections. Two tyres suitable for a Humber Hawk were produced, but about ten minutes before the start Harper decided that to mix these with SPs on the front would probably make the last state worse than the first and they popped them back into the Dunlop van.

From this point onwards the story is to take on a slightly more personal note since the author then became navigator to the service team 'B' and was able to observe the rest of the competition only through these self-imposed blinkers.

We went down on to the promenade to say 'good-bye and good luck' to all the members of the team as they came up to the ramp, and also to listen with careful ears to the remarks of the commentator to see that he said what we regarded as the right thing. It was already dark, but the Rootes team as a general rule have a little light on top of the roof showing white to the front and red to the back, which makes them mercifully easy to distinguish in the middle of the night. We were able to make these farewells since our first port of call was somewhere around in Dumfries in the early hours of the following morning, team 'C' with Lewis Garrad going to Keswick and team 'A' under the command of Gerry Spencer, one of the senior mechanics in the competition department, to Carlisle.

We, therefore, set off from Blackpool with some time in hand while the later members of the Rally were still leaving and went straight up the main road through Carlisle to find our rendezvous. It had been decided before the event that each team would not in fact be content to stay at the rendezvous originally listed (which was usually the first sizeable place after a special section) but would move backwards into the countryside and endeavour to station itself as near as possible to the end of each special section, so that if anybody had broken some vital part—even if it were only a light bulb—it could be put back at the earliest possible oppor-

SERVICE ARRANGEMENTS FOR
RAC INTERNATIONAL RALLY, NOVEMBER 1963
ROOTES SERVICE TEAM A

Gerry Spencer (Top Mechanic) Dick Wright   George Coles
Service Points will be covered as follows:

Place	Date	Approximate Time
Carlisle	11.11.63	Midnight
Lochearnhead	12.11.63	11.34
Alston	13.11.63	10.15
Blackpool	13.11.63	16.00
Bala	14.11.63	15.00
Builth Wells	14.11.63	Midnight
Bristol	15.11.63	05.30
Wareham	15.11.63	12.45
Bournemouth	15.11.63	19.30

ROOTES SERVICE TEAM B

John Rowe   Robin McDowell   Jack Walton

Newton Stewart	12.11.63	02.00
Turnberry	12.11.63	05.00
Brodie	12.11.63	19.20
Peebles	13.11.63	04.45
Blackpool	13.11.63	16.00
Trawsfynydd	14.11.63	
Llangurig	14.11.63	20.00
Williton	15.11.63	
Bournemouth	15.11.63	19.30

ROOTES SERVICE TEAM C

Lewis Garrad   John Gough (Engineering)   Johnny Butcher

Keswick	11.11.63	22.00
Keith		
Perth	13.11.63	00.12
Keswick	13.11.63	
Blackpool	13.11.63	16.00
Oulton Park	14.11.63	11.00
Machynlleth	14.11.63	19.00
Cross Gates	15.11.63	12.30
Exford	15.11.63	
Bournemouth	15.11.63	19.30

6

ROOTES SERVICE TEAM D
Norman Garrad   Ernie Beck (Mechanic)

Turnberry	12.11.63	05.00
Peebles	13.11.63	04.45
Blackpool	13.11.63	16.00
Bristol	15.11.63	05.30
Bournemouth	15.11.63	19.30

chapter 7 **Is It Really Worth It?**

Opinions have always varied as to whether racing improves the breed or the breed improves the racing. Alec Issigonis for one has always held the view that it is only the breed that improves the racing; whether he would argue the same on the score of rallies is perhaps the subject of another book. One thing is certain, however, and that is that the Sunbeam Talbot hierarchy, whether you go back to Coatalen and Roesch, or whether you pass through Bernard Winter and his successor, Peter Ware, who today holds sway, there can be no doubt that Sunbeam Talbot have always believed that intense competition in international rallies—particularly the Monte Carlo and the Alpine—produces results which are not obtainable from any other form of development testing.

Within the general framework of this statement a great variety of different attitudes is to be found and over the years various members of the Rootes Organisation have committed themselves to paper on one or more aspects of this development as they see it, and it is a most interesting sidelight on the contents of this book as a whole to see these different views.

When he was still Sir William, Lord Rootes wrote:

The Value of Rallies
Scene one is a quiet suburb of Stockholm. Mrs Ericson is setting out in her husband's car on a safe, sedate Saturday afternoon shopping expedition.

Scene two is set high in an Alpine pass. Sheila van Damm, champion European woman driver, is at the wheel of a competition Sunbeam, hurrying south at a high speed along a dangerous, ice-surfaced road in the Monte Carlo Rally.

The connection between the two? Very real and close—for it is Miss van Damm and her rally co-drivers who are continually helping to keep that shopping trip of Mrs Ericson's so safe and sedate.

More and more motor manufacturers are now coming to regard entry in international rallies as an essential part of the testing programme for their products.

Before any new model is brought on to the market, of course, it is tested and punished until it is as perfect as its manufacturer can make it. No company these days can afford to present a new car to the public until it has been proved by many months of gruelling testing.

In the Midlands of England there is a new testing ground, operated by the Motor Industry Research Association, where some of the worst road conditions in the world are reproduced. Nearly every prototype of a new British car is punished extensively here before it eventually leaves the factories as a production model. This preoccupation for perfection is a characteristic of British motor car production methods.

Whatever care a manufacturer takes, however—and modern standards are amazingly high—any new, large-production car must always remain something of an enigma until it has been sold and driven in large quantities.

It is by entering a new car in competitive events after its introduction that the manufacturer can not only prove to the world how much better it is than its competitors, but can also continue to probe to find weaknesses and make improvements. International rallies offer a fine opportunity for this, because—unlike motor racing—even the smallest family saloon can be entered and can prove its merit.

It was my own group, just after the end of the war, which pioneered the return of British manufacturers to rally motoring. Tentatively, we entered our models in these early post-war rallies. The thrashing they received over some of the worst roads on the Continent when being driven hard under the unique and stimulating urge of competition, soon revealed certain weaknesses which had eluded our experts working on the test track at home.

The lessons that we learnt then resulted in cars which were not only more efficient but were even safer for the normal motorist—people like Mrs Ericson. We are still entering rallies and we are still learning lessons, although the faults we find are very much fewer and rather more obscure these days.

The benefits of rallies, however, are not only confined to motor car manufacturers. Rally experiences have resulted in advances in the quality of motor accessories.

Headlights are now more reliable and dipping mechanisms are much more effective; spotlights are now being marketed which are calculated to do one job supremely well, whether it be cutting through fog, throwing a long, needle-like beam for fast night driving, or merely adding to the efficiency of headlights; windscreen wipers are no longer the rather unreliable instruments of the past and can be operated at differing speeds; and even the grouping of the instrument panel helps the modern driver to be a safe driver.

My own competitions manager, Mr Norman Garrad, who has himself driven in about 200 international rallies since 1923, works very closely with the leading British accessory manufacturers. From his vast experience, which he is continually supplementing by lone testing runs across the Continent, he is able to tell them just what his car needs. It was he, I remember, who was instrumental in prompting the introduction of a spotlight of a particular type a few years ago. This spotlight, which is a boon for fast driving in open country, is now in common use throughout the world. (Mrs Ericson probably has one fitted to her front fender.)

It would be untrue, of course, to say that manufacturers only enter rallies to use them for testing purposes. In these days of fierce competition, publicity is an essential part of salesmanship— and a win or even a place in one of the larger Continental rallies can bring handsome returns in the form of publicity.

A top ranking rally, like the Monte Carlo or the Midnight Sun, providing as it does the most searching trial for any car, is really a shop window facing out on to the roads of the world. A success can bring a well-earned reward, for everyone will know about it. But by the same token, an abject failure can do great harm to sales —although it may only have been caused by a cruel twist of fate.

A manufacturer, then, takes a big risk whenever he enters a car or a team. But when he does, that in itself is an indication to the motoring public that he has faith in his car.

It is a gamble which we in the Rootes Group have never avoided. To us, rallies are much too valuable a means of improving our product to ignore. And, anyway, they are such fun. . . .

This rather frank statement perhaps underplays the engineering aspect, but does at least make open admission of the benefits accrued from the kind of publicity which success in these events achieves, and anyone will tell you that there are a number of well-known European cars which would not have the market they do in Great Britain had they not been able to blow their own trumpets about their successes abroad. And the converse of this is possibly true in relation to Rootes products in America. However, you cannot win international rallies, no matter how much you need the publicity, unless you can approach the thing from an engineering point of view, and the following paper from J. J. W. Penrose, dated 12 September 1958, is not without interest:

Some Notes Illustrating How Participation in Rallies Helps the Development of the Standard Product

(A) To the ordinary motorist who seldom covers more than 300 miles in a day, any shortcomings in the comfort of the seats or the disposition and action of the controls will probably be little more than a source of minor irritation. It is possible that he may be unconscious of the fact that things are not as good as they might be in this respect but, whether he knows it or not, any defects of this sort will make him that little more tired and that little less efficient as a driver.

The same applies to the Rally driver but to a far greater extent so that it is in long distance rallies that these important details come to light. An often used but awkwardly placed control or one that is stiff to operate can become a very serious handicap after several consecutive days and nights at the wheel. An incorrectly shaped seat which at first appears to be merely a little less than really comfortable, can become an instrument of torture with 3,000 non-stop miles.

To quote an actual example, early Sunbeam Rapiers had the overdrive switch mounted on the facia panel. The incessant use of this switch in Rallies when climbing or descending an Alpine pass at high speed soon showed it was not ideally placed. It was therefore on the 'Works' Rally cars that this switch was first repositioned in the place where it is to be found today on all production Rapiers fitted with an overdrive.

As an even more important example, although the steering column gear lever was then giving every satisfaction on the standard Rapier, the competitions section at the factory proved that a floor mounted gear lever allowed even quicker and more positive gear changing giving a worthwhile advantage in timed hill climbs and speed tests. This type of control was therefore developed for the Rally cars and has since been adopted as standard on Series II Rapiers.

(B) Today many owners carry out their own maintenance work and all too often this has to be done without the help of the specialized equipment used by large garages.

The Rally driver often finds himself in the same position but with the added difficulty that any essential work must be carried out in the shortest possible time if vital marks are not to be lost through arriving late at the next control.

From both points of view, it is important that routine maintenance must be simplified as far as possible. To quote a few of the more obvious examples of how this principle has been applied in practice, it is only necessary to mention the reduction in the number of greasing points, the ease with which the level of the oil in the gear box can be checked and topped up, the accessible battery mounting, the small effort required in jacking up the car and the simplicity of the brake adjustment through the wheel and brakedrum.

(C) Long before the two-speed screen wiper was standardized for production, it had been proved on Sunbeam Mark III Rally cars to be invaluable in very heavy rain or snow.

(D) The development of braking systems to their present high standard owes much to the lessons learned in competitions. The brake lining manufacturers, whose representatives follow all the international Rallies in order to get experience at first hand, have developed linings which have a remarkable endurance and freedom from vices such as fade, grabbing, susceptibility to water or loss of power.

In the case of the group range, ribbed brake drums to assist cooling were developed for the competition cars before receiving general acceptance for production. It was competition experience, also, which showed that weight transference under heavy braking increased the front tyre adhesion to such an extent that larger brake drums could be used at the front than at the rear without danger of locking the wheels. This, of course, has now been applied to the Series II Rapier which uses ten-inch drums at the front while retaining the original nine-inch drums at the rear.

(E) Rally regulations are usually framed so that major modifications to the engine are not permitted but competition work has stimulated remarkable developments in engine performance in spite of this.

The first obvious step was to increase the capacity and this was followed by a gradual increase in compression ratio from 6·45 to 8·0 on the competition cars. Over this period the continual development of ignition equipment, air cleaners, exhaust systems and so on was continued and, as a general rule, the results were finally proved in Rallies before being passed for production. Twin carburettor layouts were first designed for Rally cars and, as a direct result of the experience gained on the earlier model, this layout has now been adopted for the standard Sunbeam Rapier.

A similar picture is painted by a short letter from Peter Ware, the present director of engineering, to a well-known motoring journalist:

I promised to send you a few examples of where our efforts in Rally and Track work had had a direct bearing on the engineering of standard production cars. None of the examples I quote are particularly spectacular, but do represent genuine findings.

Firstly, I might mention that we found out as a result of our endeavours in the African Safari Rally that our standard pave test was not as severe as might be encountered during high speed motoring in African territories. We therefore tailored our pave test to produce the type of failure encountered in the Safari and on customers' cars in East African territories.

Individual changes which can be quoted are as follows:

We recently introduced a heavier anti-roll bar on the Rapier front suspension. This has made quite a major change in handling qualities, and was the direct result of development work on the Rapier for Track racing.

We have found a weakness in the half-shaft rear hub assembly as a direct result of the Track racing.

We have shown up very quickly weaknesses on carburettor linkages as a result of Track racing.

We have carried out body reinforcement work following failures encountered in the Safari Rally.

Numerous features like petrol pipe runs and wiring failures have been changed as a result of trouble in Rallies.

Rally work makes heavy demands on the brakes, and we have obtained valuable information on pad life as a result of these conditions.

The entry of the Alpines for the Le Mans event has given us quite a bit of useful information, in particular the behaviour of individual engine components at continuous high speed operation.

As I think I described to you when you visited us here, we have made some important changes to the front suspension cross member as a direct result of experiences in the Safari Rally.

I hope this will give you an idea of typical examples which show without question that competition work does improve the breed, although naturally there are certain requirements for competition work which have no bearing on the normal touring car.

Lastly, of course, there is the point of view of the man who has to make it happen, who has to keep the drivers from each other's throats and the bits from falling off the cars. It is not always a rewarding task for success does not attend every time. It is, however, a stimulating business, beautifully summed up by Norman Garrad, who says:

Motor rallies are rather like teenage dance crazes—outwardly each one looks different, but basically they are all the same. There is more than a touch of the Black Bottom about Rock 'n Roll. And though there may appear to be a world of difference between the Coronation Safari Rally and the Monte Carlo Rally, the same elemental rules apply to each.

The 200 rallies in which I have competed since 1923 have taught me to follow the same basic rules in preparing for every international event. Whether the route lies over Alpine passes or across the plains of Uganda, the same principles apply.

Here is the formula I have evolved:

Before anything else is done, I study the rules of the competition extremely carefully. This is far more important than it sounds, particularly if the event is of an international nature and is being organised by a foreign club, for on the interpretation of a minor point in the regulations may hinge complete success or failure. It is essential to know exactly how far one can go legitimately—in fact, a team manager must become a bit of a barrack-room lawyer.

The next step is to fix a starting point for my team, whenever a choice is allowed by the organisers. The aim is to try and take most of the bad roads early in the rally before the drivers are heavy with fatigue. This involves very careful map study.

Then I choose my team. The ideal is a party of seasoned, long-distance drivers—a team which is neither too young nor too old. I always want a driver who can be relied upon to go quickly, coolly and yet safely. The fastest and most courageous driver in the world is no good to his team if he puts his car off the road. Road-care is as important on a rally route as it is on the High Street on a busy Saturday afternoon.

The next step is perhaps the most important. Every rally route should be as thoroughly reconnoitred as possible before ever a car leaves the garage. From the reconnaissance, which often takes me as long as a couple of weeks or more, I draw up a route card for each driver, detailing each section of the route and giving him instructions on how to tackle it. Some sections of the Monte Carlo rally route, for instance, are marked 'G.L.H.' on my drivers' route cards. There, they know they must Go Like Hell. Sometimes, I even mark a bump in the road!

Back from the recce, I hold a briefing with the team. This first meeting is all-important, because it is there that I give my drivers the first real picture of the route as I see it. I try to make it a picture in which the details stand out clear and sharp—it is vital, for instance, for every driver to know exactly where he must pick up his petrol. When you are driving over mountain ranges, filling stations don't come at every crossroads.

From my reconnaissance and the briefing meeting, the plan of campaign for the attack on the rally trophy really takes shape. It is then that we get down to the 101 problems that need solving before the starting day.

In consultation with the skipper of each car, I decide which driver shall tackle each section. The cars, of course, will already have been undergoing tests and alterations for several months before the rally, for—and this is a motto which might almost be engraved on my number plates—an ill-prepared car will never finish the course.

Perhaps the biggest technical problem on a rally involving high mountain travel in Europe—and so many do nowadays—is keeping perfectly clear vision for the driver. This means a constant battle against ice. The Sunbeam, which has won itself a reputation over the last seven years for being the best rally car in the world, is now thoroughly equipped to meet the ice threat. We have evolved a method of keeping the windscreen completely clear of ice however cold the temperature.

Conversely, in hot countries, the main problem, as readers will know, is keeping down the under-bonnet temperature. This can also apply at high altitudes, where the rays of the sun slicing through the thin mountain air can bring on all sort of vaporisation problems. These troubles can be avoided or minimised by fitting louvres at the side of the bonnet, lagging the petrol pipes to prevent petrol vaporisation and by placing the coil in a cold air duct.

The weather can be as hot as a foundry furnace or as cold as Christmas snow, but the rally driver's main enemy remains the same—fatigue.

Very rarely, on a tough rally, is there time to stop and take a knife and fork meal, so for most of the time the motto must be 'eat as you go'. These are the sort of provisions I like to take in my own rally car: a Thermos flask each of coffee and orange juice; glucose tablets and concentrated meat tablets; perhaps a little milk chocolate—too much can make one terribly thirsty; self-heating tins of 'commando-style' soup, with a funnel fitting for drinking at the wheel, and 'iron rations' of cooked, sliced chicken and sweets.

Cat-naps can be life savers on a long rally and blessed is the competitor who can 'sleep on a clothes line'. One tip to aid the off-duty driver is to fit curtains behind the front seat so that he can leave his worries in the driver's seat and have no distractions in the back. Stirling Moss, with whom I have driven in many rallies, always insists on having the side windows curtained too.

A team manager must also be something of a nurse-maid to his team. It is part of his responsibility to ensure that his drivers, co-drivers and navigators are fit men and women at the off. I always make sure during the three or four days that my team is travelling to the starting point for a big rally like the Monte Carlo that they are in bed early. In fact I sometimes actually tuck them up!

But do not get the impression that rally competition work is a completely cold, commercial proposition. It is impossible to mix with and to compete against men and women who love motor cars without having a lot of fun.

And that goes for rallies wherever they are held—the Trossachs, or Tyrol or Tanganyika.

. . . or Tanganyika. Peter Jopp and Gerry Alexander in their Hillman Husky successfully fording a jungle stream during the East African Coronation Safari Rally

*1964 Monte: the author's Hillman Imp in the Competition Department
at Coventry before being shipped to Minsk for the start of the rally*

*The special facia of a Hillman Imp looks more like the instrument panel
of an aircraft than that of a car*

The author and Gerry Burgess in sight of a hot bath and bed

Norman Garrad

As this book goes to Press Norman Garrad, who has been the presiding genius over almost every event and happening described in the book, has left the Rootes competition department to take on larger responsibilities within the Group.

As he leaves, the Sunbeam Rapier begins to be supplanted by new cars, and both the Imp and the new V8 Sunbeam seem to have rosy futures in the world of competition.

Marcus Chambers, already more than well known in the world of motoring competition, takes over the department—and the best of British good luck to him too!

Ave et valete.

MAJOR SUNBEAM SUCCESSES

Year	Event	Placing
1952	Monte Carlo Rally	2nd irrespective of class
	Alpine Rally	3 Coupes des Alpes
		1st, 2nd, 3rd, 4th 2–3 litre class
		Manufacturers' team prize
		1st Acceleration and Braking Test, 2–3 litre class
		Special Award
		RAC Dewar Trophy (most outstanding engineering and technical achievement)
1953	Monte Carlo Rally	Team Prize (Charles Faroux Trophy)
	Alpine Rally	4 Coupes des Alpes
		Coupe des Dames
	Great American Mountain Rally	Team Prize
	RAC Rally	Coupe des Dames
	Victorian Alpine Rally—Australia	Outright winner
1954	Monte Carlo Rally	Team Prize (Charles Faroux Trophy)
		Coupe de la Ville de Castellane— awarded to Stirling Moss for the fastest time of any car over the Col des Lacques. Speed 63·436 kph
	Alpine Rally	Gold Cup
		Coupe des Dames
		Miss Sheila van Damm was 1st in the Acceleration and Braking Test. (2000–2600 cc class)
	Great American Mountain Rally	Team Prize
	Tulip Rally	Coupe des Dames
	Geneva Rally	Coupe des Dames
	Viking Rally	Coupe des Dames
	Austrian Alpine Rally	Coupe des Dames
1955	Monte Carlo Rally	Outright winner
		Coupe des Dames

Year	Event	Placing
	RAC Rally *Daily Express* National Motor Rally	L'Equipe Cup (Best three cars of same make) Viking Challenge Cup Norwegian Cup 'L'Officiel de la Couture' Cup Coupe des Dames Coupe des Dames
1956	Monte Carlo Rally	Team Prize (Won for third time)—Outright win, Charles Faroux Trophy
	Mille Miglia	1st and 2nd Classifica Gruppe Vetture di Serie Speciale Classe 1600 cc. Achieved by the new Sunbeam Rapier competing in its first international event. Two cars entered, two cars placed
	Tulip Rally	1st (1300–1600 cc class)—Sunbeam Rapier. Four cars entered and finished in first nine
	Alpine Rally	Normal Series Production Touring Cars 1st—irrespective of class 1st—2000–2600 cc class 1st—1300–1600 cc class
1957	Mille Miglia	2nd—1300–1600 cc Special Touring Category—Sunbeam Rapier
	Tulip Rally	1st—1300–1600 cc class—Sunbeam Rapier
	Malayan Mobilgas Economy Run	Outright winner—Sunbeam Rapier
1958	Monte Carlo Rally	Stuart Trophy (Highest placed British car—Sunbeam Rapier)
	RAC International British Rally	Outright winner—achieved by Series II Sunbeam Rapier competing in its first international event
	Scottish Rally	1st and 3rd places in the Group of 2600 cc for modified Touring cars
	Circuit of Ireland International Rally	1st and 2nd in class—1300–1600 cc, Sunbeam Rapier

Year	Event	Placing
	Tulip Rally	Manufacturers' Team Prize
	Alpine Rally	1st, 2nd, 4th and 5th in the 1300–1600 cc class
		1st Coupe des Alpes
		3rd place Coupe des Dames
	Mount Elgon Rally, Uganda	Outright win and class win
1959	Monte Carlo Rally	Stuart Trophy (Highest placed British car), Sunbeam Rapier
	Alpine Rally	2 Coupes des Alpes
		1st, 2nd, 3rd, 4th and 5th in the 1300–1600 cc class
	Liège–Rome–Liège Rally	1st in class—1300–1600 cc
1960	Monte Carlo Rally	1st, 2nd, 4th in class, 1300–2000 cc
		Highest placed British car
		Class win for Alpine (Grand Touring)
	Tour of Ireland	1st, 2nd, 4th and 6th in their class (1300 cc)
		3rd in class for Sunbeam Alpine (Grand Touring over 1300 cc)
	Acropolis Rally	1st, 2nd in class
		Acropolis Cup for class victory (1300–1600 cc standard touring cars)
		NSC Cup for being 3rd of 85 starters
	International Alpine Rally	1st, 2nd, 3rd, 5th and 6th in their class, 1300–1600 cc
		2nd in Ladies' Cup
		3rd, Sunbeam Alpine in Grand Touring class
		Also 3rd in Ladies' Cup
	International Production Touring Car Race (Silverstone)	1st in 1000–1600 cc class
		Placed 6th in overall classification
	Farningham Trophy Race	6th place overall and 1st in the 1000–1600 cc production saloon car class
	International Compact Car Race USA	US Grand Prix Meeting, Riverside, California

7

Year	Event	Placing
		1st in class up to 1600 cc 3rd overall in race
1961	Mexico's Major Race Meeting of the Year	1st and 2nd places for Sunbeam Rapiers in class 1300–1600 cc
	Monte Carlo Rally	1st and 2nd places in class 1300–1600 cc Class win for Alpine 1300–2000 cc (Grand Touring)
	East African Safari	Sunbeam Rapier is 1st in class (C)
	Circuit of Ireland International Rally	Won outright in a Sunbeam Rapier
	Pietermaritzburg (Natal) Easter Meeting	1st in its class (Alpine) in 1000–1300 cc sports and production race
	International Trophy Meeting (Silverstone)	Sunbeam Rapier 1st and 3rd in its class 1000–2000 cc
	International Greek Acropolis Rally	Three Sunbeam Rapiers won the Manufacturers' Team Prize Sunbeam Rapiers 5th, 6th and 9th places
	International Scottish Rally	Outright win for Sunbeam Alpine 1st in class for Grand Touring cars over 1300 cc Sunbeam Rapier won class for Improved Touring cars over 1300 cc
	24 Hours Grand Prix at Le Mans	Sunbeam Alpine won the Index of Thermal Efficiency Cup
	International Alpine Rally	Manufacturers' Team Prize. (Challenge de l'ACMP—previously won in 1949 and 1952—for best team of three foreign cars) Challenge Team de Marque ACMP (Best team irrespective of size, class or nationality) Gatsonides Trophy. (Team of three cars, same make, recording best time in special tests) General Classification—Series Production Touring Cars—1st, 2nd and 3rd Class Awards (1300–1600 cc)—1st, 2nd and 3rd

Year	Event	Placing
	British Empire Trophy Meeting (Silverstone)	1st in 1000–1600 cc class—Production Touring Car race (Rapier)
	Three Hours' Endurance Race	3rd place overall for sports cars at Riverside, Los Angeles, California (Sunbeam Alpine)
	RAC Rally	Team Prize and 3rd and 4th places in the overall Rally 1st, 2nd and 5th in 1000–1600 cc class, with the privately entered Rapier in 4th place
1962	Monte Carlo Rally	After their brilliant performances in the Monte Carlo Rally, Sunbeam Rapier crews brought back to Britain a total of nine awards. The full Sunbeam Honours list is as follows: *Charles Faroux Trophy** (Manufacturers' Team Prize)—P. Hopkirk/P. Procter/P. Harper *Challenge Equipe* (Highest placed three cars of the same make)—P. Hopkirk/P. Procter/G. Hill *Riviera Cup* (Winner 1300–1600 cc class)—P. Hopkirk *Royal Automobile Club Trophy* (Best performance by member)—P. Hopkirk *British Automobile Racing Club Cup* (Best performance by member)—P. Procter *British Trials and Rally Drivers' Association Trophy* (Best performance by member)—P. Harper *Challenge Antony Noghes* (Best performance by competitor who has taken part in at least ten Monte Carlo Rallies)—P. Harper

* The Charles Faroux Trophy was presented in 1957 by Lord Rootes, Chairman of the Rootes Group, after the previous Trophy had been won outright by the Sunbeam team.

Year	Event	Placing
		Autosport Trophy (Best performance in a privately owned British car)—Dr J. T. Spare *First Prize—Speed and Manoeuvrability Trials* P. Hopkirk
	Circuit of Ireland Rally .	Won outright in a Sunbeam Rapier by Paddy Hopkirk, for the second year in succession. There were four awards: *The Ulster Automobile Club Trophy* *The Lombank Club Trophy* *The Autosport Trophy* *The Down Trophy* for taking first place in the 1200–1600 cc Production Touring Car Class
	Silverstone International Production Touring Car Race	1st P. Harper (Rapier) 1000–2000 cc class 2nd P. Pilsworth (Rapier) 3rd P. Jopp (Rapier) 4th E. W. Cuff-Miller (Rapier)
	Belgium Grand Prix de Spa (Spa–Francorchamps Circuit) Improved Touring Car Race	1st Lucien Bianchi (Rapier) at 95·9 mph 2nd P. Jopp (Rapier) 5th E. W. Cuff-Miller (Rapier) 6th Vic Heylen (Rapier)
	Acropolis Rally	1st place in the 1300–1600 cc class for Production Touring Cars in the 2,000 miles event, S. Zannos 2nd place Rosemary Smith and Rosemary Seers in the class, making this the second year in succession that Sunbeams have won their class
	Canary Islands	In Tenerife, J. Arias Guedes, driving a Sunbeam Rapier, won outright the city's first closed circuit national race
	Canada	In Mosport, twenty-five-year-old Eppie Wietzes won his class in a Sunbeam Alpine in the feature event of the British Empire Club's Trophy
	Crystal Palace Meeting on	1st P. Harper (Rapier) 1000–3000 cc class

Year	Event	Placing
	Whit Monday (Organised by the British Automobile Racing Club)	4th in overall classification — P. Harper Fastest lap at 69·69 mph was a new record for the class. His race average of 68·41 mph was also a race record for the class
	Scottish International Rally	1st Andrew Cowan and David Thompson (Rapier). They completed the sections in the Torlundy Forest within sixteen seconds of the fastest time of any competitor Cowan also won the class for 1000–2000 cc touring cars
	Aintree Touring Car Race 17 laps, 51 miles	1st P. Harper (Rapier) 1000–3000 cc class. His average speed was 71·84 mph (115·62 kph). He also established a new lap record for cars in the 1000–1600 cc class, lapping at 2 mins. 26·8 secs. (73·57 mph, 118·40 kph) which is a lap time a full 3 secs. faster than the previous record for the class held jointly by P. Harper and A. Hutcheson 2nd in the class—P. Jopp (Rapier) entered by Alan Fraser 4th in the class — P. Pilsworth (Rapier) entered by Alan Fraser
	Brands Hatch Molyslip Trophy Race for Touring Cars 30 laps, 79·5 miles	1st P. Jopp (Rapier) 66·4 mph, 1000–2000 cc clsss 3rd P. Harper (Rapier) Fastest lap—Harper at 68·93 mph
	Oulton Park Saloon Car Race 19 laps, 50 miles	1st P. Harper (Rapier) 75·39 mph 1000–2000 cc class P. Harper and A. Hutcheson 3rd E. W. Cuff-Miller (Rapier)
	British Racing and Sports Car Club's 1962 Saloon Car Championship	1st P. Harper (Rapier), 1000–2000 cc class 2nd P. Jopp (Rapier)
	11th Automobile Tour de France	Standard Touring Cars, 1300–1600 cc class 1st Keith Ballisat and 'Tiny' Lewis (Sunbeam Rapier)

Year	Event	Placing
	Brands Hatch International 6-Hour Saloon Car Race	2nd Peter Harper and Peter Procter (Sunbeam Rapier) 3rd Rosemary Smith and Rosemary Seers (Sunbeam Rapier) Sunbeam Rapiers finished 2nd in the Manufacturers' Team Award Coupe des Dames 1st Rosemary Smith and Rosemary Seers, also 1st Ladies' prize (Touring Cars handicap) 1300–1600 cc class 1st P. Harper/P. Procter (Rapier) 71·36 mph 2nd P. Jopp/P. Pilsworth (Rapier) 70·75 mph These cars also finished 4th and 7th respectively in overall classification
	RAC International Rally	1000–1600 cc class 1st I. D. 'Tiny' Lewis/David Mabbs (Rapier) 2nd D. E. Pollard/J. A. Baines 'Tiny' Lewis/David Mabbs also 4th in overall classification
1963	Monte Carlo Rally	*Country Club Cup* (Winner 1300–1600 cc class Production Touring Cars): Peter Harper/Ian Hall (Rapier) *Challenge Antony Noghes* (Best performance by a competitor who has taken part in at least ten Monte Carlo Rallies): Peter Harper (Rapier) for second year in succession *Challenge of the Automobil Club von Deutschland* (Best competitor starting from Germany): Peter Harper/Ian Hall (Rapier)

PREPARATION SCHEDULES

WORKS SPECIFICATION FOR PREPARATION OF SUNBEAM RAPIER CARS

ENGINE

1 Decarbonise, grind in valves and fit new valve springs.
2 Examine big end and centre main bearings.
3 Drill and wire four bolts holding gearbox to bellhousing.
4 Careful check of engine and gearbox for oil leaks.
5 Whilst head is removed for decoking, polish all ports.
6 Whilst head is removed, cut down protruding portion of inlet valve guides level with the boss inside the port.
7 Performance test engine, setting ignition timing to best advantage.
8 Fit new Champion N.5 sparking plugs (clearance 0·025).

REAR AXLE

1 Remove brake drums and examine oil seals to make sure oil is not leaking through on to the brake shoes.
2 If possible, manufacture steel blocks in place of mounting rubbers (Part No. P.79686 upper and P.79688 lower). This being done to exclude possibility of rubbers collapsing and leaving U bolts loose. This is merely a desirable precaution, not an absolute necessity.

STEERING AND FRONT SUSPENSION

1 Fit lock nuts to steering column to chassis fixing bolt.
2 Fit lock nuts to idler lever assembly bracket to chassis.
3 Examine front hub races and carefully pack front hubs with retinex 'A' grease, care being taken not to overpack the hubs i.e. no higher than the level of the smaller diameter of the outer tracks of both bearings.

PETROL SYSTEM

1 Make up and fit petrol tank undershield
2 Incorporate flexible pipe between carburettors and petrol pump.

BRAKES

1 Examine, especially for lining wear—reline if necessary.
2 These brake linings should be just bedded at the start of event, leaving maximum lining thickness for use during Rally.

COOLING SYSTEM

1 Fit Jubilee clips to all water hoses.
2 Fit radiator blind if considered necessary.
3 Add anti-freeze to radiator as required.

LIGHTING AND ELECTRICAL SYSTEM

1 Whole system checked over by expert electrician.

2 Fit foglamps, reverse lamps, etc. as considered necessary by competitor.

3 Fit under bonnet light.

4 Fit strip defrosters to windscreen if considered necessary.

5 Fit map light to facia in front of passenger seat if required by navigator.

6 Protect wiring under chassis and wings with protective sleeving against dampness, chafing, etc.

7 Accumulator should be replaced with new unit for this event.

8 Check output of dynamo and all electrical units to ensure full working order.

INSTRUMENTS

1 Speedometer should be checked for accuracy.

2 Fit navigational aids as required by competitors.

BODY AND CONTROLS

1 Modify accelerator linkage.

2 Drill holes for gearbox support cross member *right through the floor* and secure with bolts and lock nuts instead of set pins.

3 Fit safety straps to bonnet, as added security against bonnet rising at high speed.

4 Check car for freedom from water leaks.

5 Ensure adequate supply of car and ignition keys in case of loss.

6 Make sure that all door locks function correctly.

7 Make sure all windows operate correctly and are firmly fixed.

GENERAL

1 Turning circles to be checked against standard specification.

2 Track and camber to be checked.

3 Car tested for petrol and oil consumption, and performance.

4 Comprehensive tool kit to be supplied.

5 Jack (quick lift type if possible), wheel braces, wooden blocks, to be carried, also tow rope, first aid kit, etc.

6 All nuts and bolts on entire car to be checked for tightness after road testing.

7 Lock nuts to be fitted on low tension leads on coil and distributor.

8 Additional lock nuts can be fitted where convenient for you to do so.

9 Additional exhaust system support hanger brackets should be fitted where possible to ensure that the exhaust system does not fall adrift. The car should be fully lubricated and all levels checked before departure, including battery distilled water levels. We assume drivers will check all lubrication levels, etc., at least once during the Rally and the engine oil level more frequently.

WORKS PREPARATION OF SUNBEAM RAPIER IIIA
FOR USE IN THE MONTE CARLO RALLY

ENGINE

Basically standard unit built up with selected and crack tested crankshaft and connecting rods, particular attention being paid to
balancing the reciprocating parts.

Cylinder head has ports and chambers polished and the valves ground
in. The chambers are checked for volume.

Competition camshaft as supplied with the tuning kits is fitted.

Alpine carburettors with the competition jet settings are used in
conjunction with Alpine type air cleaners with the wire wool
removed.

A flexible pipe is fitted between the petrol pump and carburettor.

The accelerator pedal linkage is strengthened at the bulkhead and
stronger joints used.

The front engine bearer plate is stiffened up.

The dynamo bracket is strengthened and crack detected and the
bolts holding it wired up.

The coil is fitted on to the wing valance.

The tuning kit distributor is fitted.

An engine stabiliser is fitted between the cylinder head and the bulkhead, another stabiliser bar being fitted between the bellhousing
and the cross member.

An oil cooler is fitted between the radiator and the grille.

A Mory radiator blind is fitted.

TRANSMISSION

A lightened flywheel is used with a standard clutch that has been
checked by Borg and Beck. The clutch slave cylinder is of the
adjustable type.

The gearbox is standard but carefully checked with regard to the fit
of splines and oil seals.

The securing bolts for the bellhousing are wired.

The overdrive is specially supplied by Laycock.

The propshaft is the all-metal type.

The differential unit is standard but with crack tested parts.

The ratio is either 4·86 or 4·44.

Baffles are welded into the axle case to prevent oil surge.

Extra oil seals are fitted inboard of the bearings.

Competition half-shafts are used with hardened hubs and longer
studs.

Distance pieces are used to pack out the wheels which have thicker
centre sections and are used with larger diameter wheel nuts.

FRONT AXLE

Crossmember welded all round the seam and bump stops welded up.

All other welds examined.

Camber bolts fitted with lock nuts.

Steering arms and levers polished and crack detected.

Front crossmember bolts carried right through chassis and Nyloc nuts fitted.

STEERING UNITS

Supplied by Burman and attached to frame with Nyloc nuts.

PETROL TANK

Twenty-gallon capacity fitted in boot above rear axle, filler protrudes through wing. Original tank removed.

CHASSIS

All welding examined and reinforced if necessary.

SHOCK ABSORBERS

Units with special stiffer settings are supplied by Armstrong Patents.

BRAKES

Hawk brake pedal fitted.

All cylinder calipers and backing plates checked.

Ferodo DSII front Pads VG95 rear linings are used.

ELECTRICAL SYSTEM

All wiring, lighting, ignition system and wipers are checked.

Two driving lights and a long range lamp are fitted on the front, together with a Helphos lamp. A reverse light is also fitted.

Sockets for a navigation lamp are provided together with a map light.

An identification light is fitted on the roof.

Two strip defrosters are fitted to front screen.

TYRES

Dunlop SP are used on normal roads and Dunlop Duraband spiked tyres are used under icy conditions.

OTHER EQUIPMENT

A laminated windscreen is fitted with a Perspex shield on the inside to deflect hot air up the screen.

A Microcell lightweight driver's seat is used and a Microcell reclining navigator's seat with headrest.

Irving safety belts are fitted.

Thermos flask holders are fitted on the back of the driver's seat.

A small tool holder is fitted to the nearside door.

Bonnet safety catches are fitted.

A shovel is fitted to the boot lid.

The normal European touring equipment is carried in the boot together with selected spares and an Epco lightweight jack.

A Halda Speed pilot and two Smith's 8-day clocks are fitted.

WORKS ENGINEERING SPECIFICATION OF SUPER SNIPE AND MINX CARS FOR USE IN THE SAFARI RALLY

SUPER SNIPE

Three cars are to be built by production, the bodies to have certain modifications to the A and D posts and the tunnel by Abbey Panels before build (see below).

ENGINE

1   The engines are to be built by production with the cylinder heads
     supplied by service. They are to be run in and power checked
     before being fitted to the cars.

2   The cylinder heads will be checked for flashing in the ports and
     inlet throat size (1·29 max. dia.) and combustion chamber
     volume (72·4 min.)

3   Re-assemble cylinder head after lapping in valves and checking
     that the exhausts are of 214-NS material, with Duplex valve
     springs (X.56080 outer X.56076 inner).

4   S.G. Iron rockers are to be fitted.

5   Carburettor settings for 4,000 ft will be provided to be fitted
     before despatch.

6   The air cleaner stay is to be fitted to assist easy removal of the tap
     for element changes.

7   Examine oil pump drive gear before despatch for scuffing.

8   Crypton Revolution counters to be fitted with red band from
     500 rpm.

9   Engines must be inhibited before despatch (i.e. waterproofed).

GEARBOX AND CLUTCH

1   Standard clutch but built specially by Borg and Beck.

2   Standard gearbox and overdrive, the latter to be vetted by Lay-
     cock. Cut out overdrive inhibitor switch.

REAR AXLE

1   To use 5·125 ratio.

2   Examine welds on the retaining brackets.

3   Oil baffles to be fitted to rear axle case arms.

4   Steel plates to be fitted in place of rubber for rear springs.

5   Breathing to be modified.

6   Check half-shafts are of the latest specification.

EXHAUST SYSTEM

1   To be modified as last year to protect from flying stones.

2   Fit Servais silencers.

COOLING

1   Radiator to use 13 lbs per square inch cap.

2   Knitted hoses to be used.

3   Jubilee clips to be used on all connections.

4   Four blades to be fitted.

5   Capillary tube type thermometer to be fitted.

6   No heater to be fitted.

SUSPENSION AND STEERING

1   Steering units to be vetted by the manufacturers.

2   Steering arms, relay levers and stub carriers to be removed and
     crack tested.

3   Stays to be fitted to the top of the steering column.

4   Crossmembers with protection plate will be supplied and will be
     fitted with steel mountings.

5   Fit front springs X.69159.

6   Retain standard 13/16 stabilizer bar.
7   Front dampers GT 10–550–100–100–420.
8   Rear springs 1,214,181 'Export' spring.
9   Rear dampers GT 10–530–70–70–340.

BRAKES

1   System to be vetted by Girling—examine possibility of moving the rear pipe run.
2   Brake pads fitted with M 33 linings. } Std.
3   Brake shoes fitted with M 22 linings. } Std.
4   Cap required over rear brake adjusters to keep out dirt.
5   Use BMC brake fluid.
6   Fit Super Snipe Series II handbrake lever.

CHASSIS AND BODY

1   Wheel studs in improved material for Nyloc nuts to be fitted.
2   Standard tread tyres with nylon casings to be used.
3   Body strengthening to A and D posts and tunnel to be done at Abbey Panels before car assembly.
4   Fit grommet at bottom of rear wings.
5   No decision was taken on the petrol tanks.

TWO MINX IIIC TO BE DRAWN FROM PRODUCTION AND MODIFIED AS UNDER

ENGINE

1   Cylinder heads to be removed and checked for flashing in the ports and compression ratio (44 cc min.).
2   Measure distance of piston below block face at TDC. Best results are obtained when this is 19–25 thou. Adjust if necessary.
3   Ensure pistons are of Hepworth and Grandage manufacture.
4   Cylinder heads to be assembled with Rapier valve springs.
5   Engine to be checked for truth.
6   Fit Vogue camshaft 1,214,538.
7   Fit 34 VN carburettor and Super Minx Mk. I air cleaner.
8   Move sump drain plug.
9   Fit Rapier oil pump with provision for Tach-drive.
10 Distributor to be supplied.
11 Both engines to be checked for output.

GEARBOX AND CLUTCH

1   Standard gearbox to be used and checked over.
2   Fit Rapier clutch.

REAR AXLE

1   Fit 4·86 ratio.
2   Weld baffles to prevent oil surge.
3   Fit tuning kit half-shafts and hubs for Nyloc nuts.

EXHAUST SYSTEM

1   Fit Singer Gazelle III exhaust system.

COOLING
1 Ensure that the radiator was made by Coventry Radiators.
2 Fit 9 lbs per square inch cap.
3 Ensure that a wax thermostat is fitted.
4 Fit BD 517–4 fan. This will require a special starter dog.
5 Fit tuning kit oil cooler.

SUSPENSION AND STEERING
1 Steering units to be vetted by manufacturer.
2 Steering arms to be crack detected and polished.
3 Fit scragged crossmembers with reinforced damper mountings.
4 Front springs 1,208,274 to be supplied.
5 Fit standard front stabiliser bar 9/16 diameter.
6 Front dampers GT 10–R340–100–100–220 B.
7 Modify wishbones for eye type dampers.
8 Bump rubber X.69535, rebound X.69358.
9 Rear springs re-cambered to lift rear by ½ inch (X.68618).
10 Fit Aeon rubbers 1,202,927.
11 Rear dampers GT 10–R360–100–90–240 B.

BRAKES AND WHEELS
1 Fit Vogue back plates on front brakes.
2 Fit VG 95 linings front and rear.
3 System to be vetted by manufacturer.
4 Fit standard tyres.

BODY
1 Insurance weld at the front.
2 Bolt front crossmember right through using cyanide hardened washers.

HARTWELL'S PREPARATION OF FACTORY SPECIFICATION 'A'—SUNBEAM RAPIER SERIES III

ENGINE
Standard unit built up with laboratory-tested parts, particular attention being paid to balance and weights of all moving parts.
Cylinder head polished and valves ground in.
Flexible petrol pipes fitted between petrol pump and carburettor.
Accelerator pedal linkage strengthened at bulkhead.
Waterproof plug covers fitted.
Coil moved from position on engine unit to wing valance.
Alpine carburettor fitted with Alpine type air cleaners.
Front engine bearer plate strengthened.
Dynamo bracket strengthened and crack tested.
Mory radiator blind fitted.

GEARBOX
Standard unit—laboratory-tested gears and shafts—with special attention being paid to oil seals.
Securing bolts on bellhousing drilled and wired.

CLUTCH

Selected unit supplied by Lockheed with heavier spring setting.

OVERDRIVE

Selected unit supplied by Laycock—modified to operate on second gear.

REAR AXLE

Standard unit—built up with laboratory-tested parts.

Welding checked on case and special oil seals fitted to half-shafts.

Rear hubs fitted with longer wheel studs to facilitate the use of Nyloc wheel nuts.

Distance pieces fitted to half-shafts to pack out the wheels from the wheel arch—to enable Weathermaster tyres to be fitted with chains and clear the wing.

Special axle breathers fitted.

FRONT AXLE

Welding on front crossmembers examined and strengthened.

Strengthening plate fitted to base of crossmember.

Camber bolts fitted with locking nuts.

Steering arms and drop arms balanced and crack tested by laboratory.

Front crossmember fixings; front pair bolted right through, pinned and fitted with self-locking nuts.

STEERING UNIT

Selected unit supplied by Burmans—with particular attention being paid to clearances.

Secured on frame with Nyloc nuts.

PETROL TANK

Fitted with drain plug and high take off point.

Petrol tank guard fitted.

CHASSIS

Welding examined and rectified as necessary.

SHOCK ABSORBERS

Selected unit supplied with stiffer settings by Armstrong Patents.

Front unit modified to eye-bolt type of fixing.

BRAKES

Hawk brake pedal fitted.

Wheel cylinders, calipers and pipes fitted and checked by Lockheed.

Competition type brake linings supplied by Ferodo—namely DS3 front and VG95 rear.

Clayton Dewandre Motovac Servo Unit fitted.

ELECTRICAL SYSTEM

All wiring, lighting, ignition system and wipers checked by Lucas—who also fitted voltage regulators—twin double dipping spot lamps, reversing lamp, two pin socket plug—headlamp flashers and Butler navigation lamp.

A Helphos sign poster lamp also fitted.

To assist in the de-icing of the windscreen a three-inch Perspex shield is fitted on the inside of the windscreen to direct hot air from the demister on to the screen.

APPENDIX III

HOMOLOGATION SCHEDULES

Manufacturers Reference No. for Application

HILLMAN SUPER MINX 1

F.I.A. Recognition No.

ROYAL AUTOMOBILE CLUB
PALL MALL, LONDON, S.W.I.

Federation Internationale de l'Automobile.

*Form of Recognition in accordance with
Appendix J to the
International Sporting Code.*

Manufacturer ROOTES GROUP

Model HILLMAN SUPER MINX 1   Year of Manufacture 1961

Serial No. of   Chassis B.1200001

Engine B.1200001

Type of Coachwork Saloon

Recognition is valid from 1st January, 1962   In category Touring

Photograph to be affixed here ¾ view of car from front right.

affixed here.

107

General description of car:

FOUR DOOR SALOON

Photographs to be affixed below.

¾ view of car from rear left.

Interior view of car through driver's door.

Engine unit with accessories from right.

Engine unit with accessories from left.

Front axle complete (without wheels).

Rear axle complete (without wheels).

ENGINE

No. of cylinders 4   in line ....
                                  box/
                                  opposed

Cycle ..... 4 Stroke   Firing order ..... 1 - 3 - 4 - 2
Capacity ..... 1592 ..... c.c.   Bore ..... 81.5 ..... m.m.   Stroke ..... 76.2 ..... m.m.
Maximum rebore ..... 82.25 mm   Resultant capacity ..... 1620 ..... c.c.
Material of cylinder block ..... Cast Iron   Material of sleeves, if fitted ..... -

Distance from crankshaft centre line to top
face of block at centre line of cylinders ..... 231.8 ..... m.m.
Material of cylinder head ..... Cast Iron   Volume of one combustion chamber ..... 44/46 ..... c.c.

Compression ratio 8.3:1
Material of piston ..... "Heplex"   No. of piston rings 3
Distance from gudgeon pin centre line to highest point of piston crown ..... 46.9 ..... m.m.

Bearings {
  Crankshaft main bearings: Type ..... White metal lined Dia. ..... 57.13 ..... m.m.
  Connecting rod big end: Type ..... Lead indium lined Dia. ..... 50.82 ..... m.m.
}

Weights {
  Flywheel ..... 9.87 ..... kg.
  Crankshaft ..... 15.42 ..... kg.
  Connecting rod ..... .71 ..... kg. with bearing shells and small end.
  Piston with rings ..... .44 ..... kg.
  Gudgeon pin ..... .14 ..... kg.
}

No. of valves per cylinder 2   Method of valve operation ..... Pushrod
No. of camshafts 1   Location of camshafts ..... cylinder block
Type of camshaft drive ..... Chaindrive from crankshaft

Diameter of valves: Inlet ..... 36.45 ..... m.m.   Exhaust ..... 29.8 ..... m.m.
Diameter of port
at valve seat: Inlet ..... 33.3 ..... m.m.   Exhaust ..... 26.9 ..... m.m.
Tappet clearance for
checking timing: Inlet ..... .5 at valve tip ..... m.m.   Exhaust ..... .5 at valve tip ..... m.m.
Valves open: Inlet ..... 14° B.T.D.C   Exhaust ..... 56° B.B.D.C
Valves close: Inlet ..... 52° A.B.D.C   Exhaust ..... 10° A.T.D.C
Maximum valve lift: Inlet ..... 8.62 ..... m.m.   Exhaust ..... 8.58 ..... m.m.

Degrees of crankshaft rotation from zero to—

Maximum lift: Inlet 123   Exhaust 123
¾ Maximum lift: Inlet 71   Exhaust 71

Valve springs: Inlet   Exhaust
            Type ..... Helical coil   Helical coil
            No. per valve 2   2
Carburettor: Type ..... Downdraught   No. fitted 1
            (up or down draft, horizontal)
Make ..... Zenith   Model ..... 32 VN
Flange hole diameter ..... 32 ..... m.m.   Choke diameter ..... 27 ..... m.m.
Main jet identification No. 65

3

Air filter: Type......Paper Element......   No. fitted......1
Inlet manifold:
   Diameter of flange hole at carburettor......33......m.m.
   Diameter of flange hole at port......32......m.m.

Photograph of combustion chamber to be affixed here.

Photograph of inlet manifold to be affixed here.

Exhaust manifold:
   Diameter of flange hole at port......27......m.m.
   Diameter of flange hole at connection to silencer inlet pipe......45.7......m.m.

Photograph of piston showing crown to be affixed here.

Photograph of exhaust manifold to be affixed here.

ENGINE ACCESSORIES

Make of fuel pump......A.C   No. fitted......1
Method of operation......Mechanical
Type of ignition system......Coil ......coil or magneto
Make of ignition......Lucas   Model......DM2
Method of advance and retard......Centrifugal and Vacuum
Make of ignition coil......Lucas   Model......HA 12
No. of ignition coils......1   Voltage......12
Make of dynamo......Lucas   Model......C40
Voltage of dynamo......12   Maximum output......19......amps.
Make of starter motor......Lucas   Model......M35G
Battery: No. fitted......1   Voltage......12   Capacity......38......amp. hour

4

SUPER MINX

Make.. HILLMAN .... Model.................... F.I.A. Recognition No.....................

Manufacturers Reference No. of Application...Hillman Super Minx 1

TRANSMISSION

Make of clutch....Borg.&.Beck................ Type Single..dry..plate...........

Diameter of clutch plate....8.0 in.......... No. of plates...1.........

Method of operating clutch....Mechanical.through.hydraulic.......

Make of gearbox....Rootes.............. Type ....Constant............

No. of gearbox ratios....4.forward.and.1.reverse.......

Method of operating gearshift............Manual.......

Location of gearshift..........Centre.floor.lever.and.column.....

Is overdrive fitted?............No....

Method of controlling overdrive, if fitted..........-

	GEARBOX RATIOS		ALTERNATIVE RATIOS					
	Ratio	No. of Teeth	Ratio	No. of Teeth	Ratio	No. of Teeth	Ratio	No. of Teeth
1.	3.346	$\frac{29}{20}\times\frac{30}{13}$						
2.	2.141	$\frac{29}{20}\times\frac{31}{21}$						
3.	1.392	$\frac{29}{20}\times\frac{24}{25}$						
4.	1.0	Direct						
Rev.5.	4.239	$\frac{29}{20}\times\frac{30}{13}\times\frac{19}{15}$						

Type of final drive............Hypoid........

Type of differential..........Normal - 2 Pinions and side gears.....

Final drive ratio..4.22:1........ Alternatives ...3.84....4.44....4.86........

No. of teeth ...9/38............ ....9/35...9/40...7/35......

Overdrive ratio, if fitted...........-

WHEELS

Type ...Pressed steel disc........... Weight.......5.75................... kg.

Method of attachment ....4 - $\frac{7}{16}$ in UNF Bolts.....

Rim diameter...330.2............. m.m. Rim width...114.3........ m.m.

Tyre size: Front6.00 x 13 .... Rear.....6.00 x 13.....

BRAKES

Method of operation .... Hydraulic........

Is servo assistance fitted?...no......

Type of servo, if fitted.........-

No. of hydraulic master cylinders ....1..... Bore ...17.8............ m.m.

	Front	Rear
No. of wheel cylinders	2.per wheel	1 per wheel
Bore of wheel cylinders	20.3 m.m.	19.1 m.m.
Inside diameter of brake drums	229 m.m.	229 m.m.
No. of shoes per brake	2	2
Outside diameter of brake discs	– m.m.	– m.m.
No. of pads per brake	–	–

Dimensions of brake linings per shoe or pad (if all shoes or pads in each brake are not of same dimensions, specify each)

	Front	Rear
Length	219 m.m.	219 m.m.
	219 m.m.	219 m.m.
Width	44.5 m.m.	44.5 m.m.
Total area per brake	19,500 m.m.^{2}	19,500 m.m.^{2}

SUSPENSION

	Front	Rear
Type	Independent	Live axle
Type of spring	Coil	Semi elliptic leaf
Is stabiliser fitted?	Yes	No
Type of shock absorber	Hydraulic telescopic	Hydraulic telescopic
No. of shock absorbers	2	2

STEERING

Type of steering gear .... Burman recirculating ball

Turning circle of car .... 10.97 .... m., approx.

No. of turns of steering wheel from lock to lock 3.2

CAPACITIES AND DIMENSIONS

Fuel tank .... 50 .... litres   Sump .... 3.9 sump only / 4.5 inc filter .... litres

Radiator & engine 7 .... litres

Overall length of car .... 419 .... cm.   Overall width of car .... 162 .... cm.

Overall height of car, unladen (with hood up, if appropriate) .... 148 .... cm.

Distance from floor to top of windscreen:

Highest point .... 104 .... cm.   Lowest point .... 101 .... cm.

Width of windscreen:

Maximum width .... 129 .... cm.   Minimum width .... 119 .... cm.

*Interior width of car .... 129.5 .... cm.

No. of seats 4/5

Track: Front 131 .... cm.   Rear .... 123 .... cm.

Wheelbase 256.5 .... cm.   Ground clearance .... 165 .... m.m.

*(To be measured at the immediate rear of the steering wheel, and the width quoted to be maintained in a vertical plane of not less than 25 cms.)

Overall weight with water, oil and spare wheel, but without fuel .... 1040 .... kgs.

Additional information for cars fitted with two-cycle engines

System of cylinder scavenging...

Type of lubrication...

Size of inlet port:

Length measured around cylinder wall...m.m.

Height..m.m.   Area...m.m.^{2}

Size of exhaust port:

Length measured around cylinder wall...m.m.

Height..m.m.   Area...m.m.^{2}

Size of transfer port:

Length measured around cylinder wall...m.m.

Height..m.m.   Area...m.m.^{2}

Size of piston port:

Length measured around piston..m.m.

Height..m.m.   Area·..m.m.^{2}

Method of pre-compression...

Bore and stroke of pre-compression cylinder, if fitted..m.m.

Distance from top of cylinder block to lowest point of inlet port..m.m.

Distance from top of cylinder block to highest point of exhaust port..m.m.

Distance from top of cylinder block to highest point of transfer port..m.m.

Drawing of cylinder ports.

Supercharger, if fitted

Make ....   Model or Type No. ....

Type of drive ....   Ratio of drive ....

Fuel injection, if fitted

Make of pump...................................   Model or Type No...

Make of injectors ....   Model or Type No...

Location of injectors...

7

Optional equipment affecting preceeding information.—

1 Petrol Tank Shield available.

2. Heavy duty suspension with Aeon Rubber Assistance available. Export countries Australia, Africa and New Zealand.

3. Long range Fuel Tank available. Capacity 100 Litres

4. Oil Cooler available

5. Electrical Petrol pump available

6. Light Weight Competitions seats available

7. Automatic Transmission.

OFFICIAL RECOGNITION OF JABBEKE RECORDS

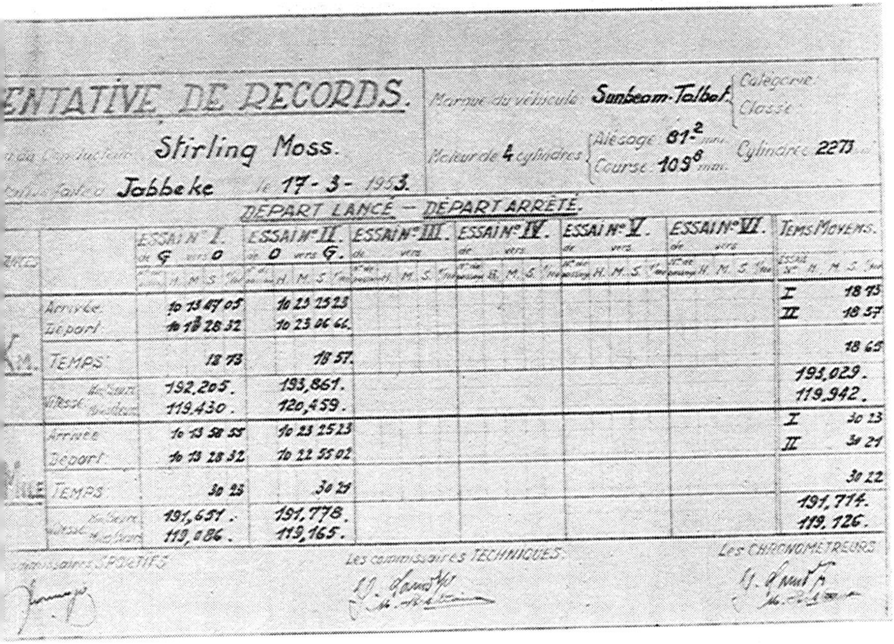

TENTATIVE DE RECORDS.

Marque du véhicule: **Sunbeam-Talbot**

Catégorie:

Classe:

Nom du Conducteur: **Sheila Van Damm**

Moteur de **4** cylindres

Alésage **81** ^{2} mm

Tentative faite à **Jobbeke** le **17-3-1953.**

Course **109** ^{8} mm.

Cylindrée **2273.**

DÉPART LANCÉ — ~~DÉPART ARRÊTÉ~~

DISTANCES		ESSAI N° I. de **C** vers 0	ESSAI N° II. de 0 vers **G**.	ESSAI N° III. de vers	ESSAI N° IV. de vers	ESSAI N° V. de vers	ESSAI N° VI. de vers	TEMPS MOYEN
		H. M. S.	H M S	H M S	H M S	H M S	H M S	ESSAI N° / H M S
1 KM.	Arrivée	11.12.37.55	11 18 48 92					I. 18
	Départ	11 12 19 67	11 18 30 35					II. 18
	TEMPS:	18 68	18 57					18
	Vitesse Km/heure	192,719.	193,861					193,340
	Vitesse Miles/heure	119. 749	120,459					120,135
1 MILE	Arrivée	11 12 48 77	11 18 48 92					I. 30
	Départ	11 12 18 67	11 18 18 72					II. 30
	TEMPS:	30 10	30 20					30
	Vitesse Km/heure	192,479.	191,841					192,160.
	Vitesse Miles/heure	119,601.	119,205.					119,401.

Les commissaires SPORTIFS:

Les commissaires TECHNIQUES:

Les CHRONOMETREURS:

ROOTES MODELS 1946–1961

With notes indicating changes and developments, together with simplified list of models with introduction dates.

HUMBER SUPER SNIPE

Year	Model	Cylinders	Wheel-base	Tyre Size	BHP and RPM	Capacity (cc)	Remarks
1946	Saloon (Snipe)	6	114"	600×16	65 @ 3500	2731·5	This model was virtually identical with the Humber Hawk 1946/7 but had a 6-cylinder power unit of 2731·5 cubic capacity. N.B. The Humber Super Snipe of 4086 cubic capacity also used this body shell. The smaller 6-cylinder was discontinued after 1947
1946/7	Saloon	6	114"	600×16	100 @ 3400	4086	This was the larger version of the 6-cylinder car mentioned above
1948/9	Saloon	6	117½"	650×16	100 @ 3400	4086	1948 saw the introduction of the new body with increased wheel base. Also the steering column gear change
1950/1	Saloon	6	117½"	650×16	100 @ 3400	4086	Detail changes only for 1950/1
1952/7	Saloon	6	115¾"	700×15	113 @ 3400 increased to 130·5 @ 3600	4138·8	Entirely new power unit introduced with overhead push rod operated valves, giving greatly increased performance. Independent front suspension altered from transverse leaf spring to coil springs. Optional overdrive and Borg Warner automatic transmission also available for this model
1958/9	Saloon	6	110"	670×15	112 @ 5000	2651	An entirely new car with body based on

Model							Notes
Estate Car	6	110"	670 × 15	to 123 @ 4900 / 112 @ 5000 / increased to 123 @ 4900	2651		synchromesh) overdrive optional on second and third. Borg Warner automatic transmission optional. Power assisted steering optional. Power assisted brakes standard. Full 6-seater with luxury appointments

HUMBER IMPERIAL AND PULLMAN

Year	Model						Notes
1945/8	Pullman Limousine	6	127½"	700 × 16	107 @ 3400	4086	7/8 passenger Limousine, similar to Super Snipe, but with larger wheelbase. Two occasional seats. Projecting boot. Sliding glass division
1948	Pullman Limousine	6	131"	700 × 16	107 @ 3400	4086	Detail changes including built-in headlights, alligator bonnet, enclosed rear wheels
1949/52	Pullman Limousine	6	131"	700 × 16	107 @ 3400	4086	Imperial introduced and Pullman continued. Detail changes only incorporated between 1949 and 1952
	Imperial Saloon	6	131"	700 × 16	107 @ 3400	4086	
1953/4	Pullman Limousine	6	131"	750 × 16	121 @ 3400	4138	Improved design fitted with ohv engine, similar to Super Snipe unit
	Imperial Saloon	6	131"	750 × 16	121 @ 3400	4138	

HUMBER HAWK

Year	Model	Cylinders	Wheel-base	Tyre Size	BHP and RPM	Capacity (cc)	Remarks
1946/7	Saloon	4	114″	575 × 16	56 @ 3800	1944	New model introduced with the same body as the Snipe but using a 4-cylinder engine developed from the 1938/40 Hillman 14
1948	Saloon	4	114″	575 × 16	56 @ 3800	1944	The only major change for 1948 was the introduction of the steering column gear change
1949	Saloon	4	105½″	550 × 15	56 @ 3800	1944	An entirely new body design introduced using the same power unit. Independent front suspension with transverse leaf spring replaced by coil springs
1950/1	Saloon	4	105½″	640 × 15 4 ply	58 @ 3400	2267	The 1950 model saw the further development of the Hawk with an increased cubic capacity and larger section tyres
1952	Saloon	4	105½″	640 × 15	58 @ 3400	2267	Detail changes only for 1952
1954/6	Saloon	4	105½″	640 × 15	70 @ 4000	2267	1954 saw the introduction of an over-head valve engine giving greatly increased power and performance. Detail body changes—push button operated door locks. Overdrive also offered. Also introduction of a new Estate Car
	Estate Car	4	105½″	640 × 15 6 ply	70 @ 4000	2267	

Year	Body	Cyl.	Wheelbase	Tyres	b.h.p. @ r.p.m.	Weight	Notes
	Estate Car	4	110"	4 ply 640 × 15 6 ply	78 @ 4400	2267	...also available for this model. A new series introduced, entirely new unit construction body, the largest of its type. Increased wheelbase—entirely new styling and instrument panel. Full 6-seater
1959	Saloon	4	110"	640 × 15	78 @ 4400	2267	Unchanged except for new style facia panel finished in burr walnut and walnut door cappings
	Estate Car	4	110"	640 × 15 6 ply	78 @ 4400	2267	

HILLMAN MINX

Year	Body	Cyl.	Wheelbase	Tyres	b.h.p. @ r.p.m.	Weight	Notes
1946/7	Saloon	4	92"	500 × 16	35 @ 4100	1184·5	
	Convertible	4	92"	500 × 16	35 @ 4100	1184·5	
	Estate Car	4	92"	525 × 16	35 @ 4100	1184·5	
1948	Saloon	4	92"	500 × 16	35 @ 4100	1184·5	1948 saw the introduction of Lockheed hydraulic brakes, steering column gear change, headlamps built into the wings
	Convertible	4	92"	500 × 16	35 @ 4100	1184·5	
	Estate Car	4	92"	525 × 16	35 @ 4100	1184·5	
1949	Saloon	4	93"	500 × 16	35 @ 4100	1184·5	1949 saw the introduction of new type body, independent front suspension, water pump
	Convertible	4	93"	500 × 16	35 @ 4100	1184·5	

Year	Model	Cylinders	Wheel-base	Tyre Size	BHP and RPM	Capacity (cc)	Remarks
1950/2	Estate Car	4	93"	550 × 15	35 @ 4100	1184·5	1950 saw the introduction of a larger bore, increasing cubic capacity from 1184·5 to 1265. Side lamps separately in wings, larger diameter headlamps
	Saloon	4	93"	500 × 16	37·5 @ 4200	1265	
	Convertible	4	93"	500 × 16	37·5 @ 4200	1265	
	Estate Car	4	93"	550 × 15	37·5 @ 4200	1265	
1953/4	Saloon	4	93"	500 × 16	37·5 @ 4200	1265	Detail changes only for 1953/4, including push-button operated door locks, new type radiator grille and surround. New hard-top coupé also introduced, known as the 'Californian', for 1954
	Convertible	4	93"	400 × 16	37·5 @ 4200	1265	
	Estate	4	93"	550 × 15	37·5 @ 4200	1265	
1955	Saloon	4	93"	560 × 15	43 @ 4400	1390	1955 saw the introduction of a new power unit, with overhead, push rod operated valves, giving increased cubic capacity to 1390 cc, also Zenith carburettor fitted in place of Solex. *Note*: Early 1955 Mark VIII were fitted with side valve engine up to the introduction of the new engine
	Convertible	4	93"	560 × 15	43 @ 4400	1390	
	Estate Car	4	93"	550 × 15	43 @ 4400	1390	
1956	Saloon	4	96"	560 × 15	51 @ 4600	1390	1956 saw the introduction of a further stage in the design of a new series, giving a longer wheelbase, new body and styling. (Known as the Series I)
	Convertible	4	96"	560 × 15	51 @ 4600	1390	
	Estate	4	96"	550 × 15	51 @ 4600	1390	

Year	Model	Cyl.	Wheelbase	Tyres	Power	Capacity	Notes
1957	Saloon	4	96"	560 × 15	51 @ 4400	1390	1957 saw a further stage in the development of the new series—minor changes only—a new high torque camshaft giving increased power. Manumatic 2-pedal control offered as optional
	Convertible	4	96"	560 × 15	51 @ 4400	1390	
	Estate Car	4	96"	550 × 15	51 @ 4400	1390	
	Special Saloon	4	96"	500 × 15	47·5 @ 4400	1390	A simplified model also introduced, with 500 × 15 tyres, central gear change and simplified instrument panel
1958/9	Saloon	4	96"	560 × 15	52·5 @ 4400	1494	Detail styling changes, engine capacity increased to $1\frac{1}{2}$ litres. New facia panel. 'Special' fitted with bench seat in place of two bucket seats
	Convertible	4	96"	560 × 15	52·5 @ 4400	1494	
	Estate Car	4	96"	550 or 590 × 15	52·5 @ 4400	1494	
	Special	4	96"	560 × 15	52·5 @ 4400	1490	

HILLMAN HUSKY

Year	Model	Cyl.	Wheelbase	Tyres	Power	Capacity	Notes
1954/7	Hillman Husky	4	84"	500 × 15	35 @ 4100	1265	A new model introduced of the Estate Car type, using the side valve Minx-type engine
1958/9	Hillman Husky	4	86"	560 × 15	43 @ 4000	1390	Further development of the Husky, new body, and using ohv engine giving more power. Also longer wheelbase and greater loading capacity

SUNBEAM ALPINE

Year	Model	Cylinders	Wheel-base	Tyre Size	BHP and RPM	Capacity (cc)	Remarks
1953/5	Sports	4	97·5"	550×16 Alpine Special	80 @ 4200 97·5 @ 4500	2267	A 2-seater sports version of the Sunbeam-Talbot 90. Overdrive optional on late models
1959	Sports	4	96"	560×15	83·5 @ 5300	1494	An entirely new 2-seater sports car with 1½-litre engine based on the Sunbeam Rapier power unit. New alloy cylinder head. Close ratio gearbox. Hypoid rear axle. Disc brakes (front) fitted to Rootes car as standard for first time. Luxury appointments (e.g. wind-up side windows). Optional extras include overdrive (on third and top gears). Hard-top and centre lock wire wheels

SUNBEAM RAPIER

Year	Model	Cylinders	Wheel-base	Tyre Size	BHP and RPM	Capacity (cc)	Remarks
1955/6	Saloon	4	96"	560×15	62 × 5000	1390	A completely new addition to the Sunbeam range. A 2-door 'hard-top' saloon with sporting characteristics. Overdrive in third and top gears. Standard equipment
1956/8	Saloon	4	96"	560×15	67·5 @ 5000	1390	R67 twin carburettor engine introduced, giving greater power output and improved performance

Year	Body	Cyl.	Wheelbase	Tyres	bhp @ rpm	cc	Remarks
1958/9	Saloon	4	96"	560 × 15	73 @ 5200	1494	New twin carburettor 'Rallymaster' 1½-litre engine introduced. Bigger brakes, improved steering and suspension. Centre-floor remote control gearchange standard. Changes to body styling included new front grille and finned rear wings. Overdrive optional. Rapier Convertible introduced
	Convertible	4	96"	560 × 15	73 @ 5200	1494	

SUNBEAM-TALBOT

Year	Body	Cyl.	Wheelbase	Tyres	bhp @ rpm	cc	Remarks
1946/7	Saloon	4	94"	525 × 16	39 @ 4400	1184·5	This model was known as the Sunbeam-Talbot Ten, and had cable operated Bendix brakes. The 2-litre model with similar body had Lockheed hydraulic brakes (see below)
	Convertible	4	94"	525 × 16	39 @ 4400	1184·5	
	Tourer	4	94"	525 × 15	30 @ 4400	1184·5	
1946/7	Saloon	4	97¾"	525 × 16	56 @ 3800	1944	This was larger version of the 'Ten' with a similar body specification and Lockheed hydraulic brakes
	Convertible	4	97¾"	525 × 16	56 @ 3800	1944	
	Tourer	4	97¾"	525 × 16	56 @ 3800	1944	
1948	Saloon	4	97½"	525 or 550 × 16	47 @ 4800	1184·5	New model of the 'Ten' introduced, known as the Sunbeam-Talbot 80. This had a new body, steering column gear change, etc. Overhead valves. The 2-litre model was also available and known as the 90. N.B. The 80 was discontinued after 1948, but the 90 continued until 1955
	Convertible	4	97½"	525 or 550 × 16	47 @ 4800	1184·5	

Year	Model	Cylinders	Wheel-base	Tyre Size	BHP and RPM	Capacity (cc)	Remarks
1948	Saloon	4	97½"	525 or 550×16	64 @ 4100	1944	New model of the 2-litre, with new body, steering column gear change, etc.
	Convertible	4	97½"	525 or 550×16	64 @ 4100	1944	
1950/1	Saloon	4	97½"	550×16	70 @ 4000	2267	Further development, increased engine size, independent front suspension with coil springs
	Convertible	4	97½"	550×16	70 @ 4000	2267	
1952/5	Saloon	4	97½"	550×16	77 @ 4100	2267	Minor changes only
	Convertible	4	97½"	550×16	77 @ 4100	2267	
1955/7	Saloon	4	97½"	550×16	80 @ 4400	2267	Further development and model name changed to Sunbeam III
	Convertible	4	97½"	550×16	80 @ 4400	2267	

SINGER

Year	Model	Cylinders	Wheel-base	Tyre Size	BHP and RPM	Capacity (cc)	Remarks
1946/8	Nine Roadster	4	91"	500×16	36 × 5000	1074	A 4-seater sports roadster fitted with a single overhead camshaft engine
1949	Nine Roadster	4	91"	500×16	36 @ 5000	1074	4-speed gearbox introduced with detail changes only
1950/2	Nine Roadster	4	91"	500×16	36 @ 5000	1074	Independent front wheel suspension introduced with disc wheels (previously semi-elliptic springs with pierced

Year	Model	Cyl.	Wheelbase	Tyres	B.H.P. @ r.p.m.	c.c.	Remarks
1946/9	Ten Saloon	4	95"	525×16	38 @ 4800	1193·5	4-door saloon. Flush boot, bucket seats, sunshine roof. Grille similar to Nine Roadster
1946/9	Twelve Saloon	4	103"	550×16	43 @ 4200	1525	Similar to Ten. Large wheel discs, cloth 'Cord' trim, protruding boot, sunshine roof
1948/50	S.M.1500 Saloon	4	107·5"	550×16	50 @ 4500	1506	A completely new model in post-war styling. All-steel body on separate chassis. IFS by coil springs
1951/4	S.M.1500 Saloon	4	107·5"	550×16	50 @ 4500	1497	Engine stroke altered to bring engine capacity below 1500 cc. Detail changes only between 1951 and 1954
1951/4	S.M. Roadster	4	91"	550×16	50 @ 4500	1497	A 4-seater sports roadster similar to the Nine, but with engine specification of the S.M.1500 saloon
1954/6	Hunter Saloon	4	107·5"	550×16	50 @ 4200	1497	A new model with body and chassis based on the S.M.1500. Traditional vertical bar radiator grille and overall luxury finish. Economy version called Hunter S. offered from September 1955. In October 1955 the Hunter 75 twin-carburettor car was announced, but did not go into mass production. Hunter de Luxe with wooden facia panel and door fillets introduced March 1956
1956	Gazelle Saloon	4	96"	560×15	53 @ 4500	1496	First completely new model resulting from Singer/Rootes merger. The well

Year	Model	Cylinders	Wheel-base	Tyre Size	BHP and RPM	Capacity cc	Remarks
	Gazelle Convertible	4	96"	560 × 15	35 @ 4500	1496	proven 1½-litre Singer ohc engine used in conjunction with other major components from the existing Rootes range combined to offer two luxury-finished models in the 1½-litre range. Walnut facia and door fillets
1957	Gazelle Saloon	4	96"	560 × 15	53 @ 4500	1496	
	Gazelle Convertible	4	96"	560 × 15	53 @ 4500	1496	Estate Car introduced to range. Overdrive on third and top gears optional. Tank capacity increased from 7·25 to 10 gallons. Detail changes to body included cowled headlights, redesigned side grills, Gazelle head bonnet motif. Contrasting colour flash on body sides
	Gazelle Estate Car	4	96"	550 × 15	53 @ 4500	1496	
1958/9	Gazelle Saloon	4	96"	560 × 15	60 @ 4500	1494	
	Gazelle Convertible	4	96"	560 × 15	60 @ 4500	1494	Ohv push rod 1½-litre engine offered as optional February 1958. Ohc engine discontinued later in 1958, when detail changes made to styling included redesigned second colour flash
	Gazelle Estate Car	4	96"	550 or 590 × 15	60 @ 4500	1494	

HILLMAN

Model	Date of Introduction
Mark I	Approx. July 1945
Mark II	December 1947
Mark III	September 1948
Mark IV	November 1949
Mark V	October 1951
Mark VI	February 1953
Mark VII	October 1953
Mark VIII	October 1954
Husky	October 1954
Minx Series I	May 1956
Series II	August 1957
Series III	September 1958
Series IIIA	September 1959
Series IIIB	August 1960
Series IIIC	August 1961
Husky Series I	January 1958
Series II	March 1960
Series II with introduction of hypoid axle	August 1960
Series II with introduction of 26 VME carburettor and 4·22 axle	November 1961
Super Minx Mark I	October 1961

HUMBER HAWK

Model	Date of Introduction
Mark I	Approx. July 1945
Mark II	September 1947
Mark III	October 1948
Mark IV	September 1950
Mark V	September 1952
Mark VI	June 1954
Series I	May 1957
Series I with wood facia	October 1958
Series IA	October 1959
Series II	October 1960

HUMBER SUPER SNIPE

Model	Date of Introduction
Mark I	Approx. July 1945
Mark II	September 1947
Mark III	August 1950
Mark IV	October 1952
Mark IV with wood cappings and facia	April 1954
Mark IVA High compression ratio	October 1955
Mark IVB Increased performance	August 1956
Super Snipe available with automatic drive	August 1956
Series I	October 1958
Series II	October 1959
Series III	October 1960

SUNBEAM

Model	Date of Introduction
10	Approx. July 1945
2-litre	
90 Mark I	June 1948
80 Mark I	
90 Mark II	September 1950
90 Mark IIA	September 1952
90 Mark IIA with high compression head	October 1953
90 Mark III	October 1954
Rapier Series I	October 1955
Alpine	March 1953
Rapier (Two carburettors)	September 1956
Series II	February 1959
Series III	September 1959
Series IIIA	April 1961
Sunbeam Alpine	July 1959
Series II	October 1960

SINGER

Model	Date of Introduction	
Gazelle Series I	September	1956
Series II	October	1957
Series IIA ohv engine		
introduced	February	1958
Series III	September	1958
Series IIIA	September	1959
Series IIIB	August	1960
Series IIIC	July	1961
Vogue Mark I	July	1961

MAP OF STIRLING MOSS'S OSLO–LISBON RUN

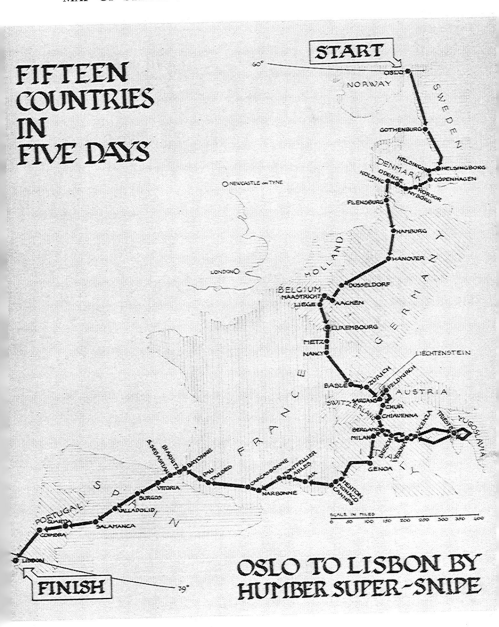

LIST OF FAMOUS DRIVERS IN THE SUNBEAM TEAM AT ONE TIME OR ANOTHER

Raymond Baxter	Paddy Hopkirk
Joachim Bonnier	Leslie Johnson
Jack Brabham	Peter Jopp
Ivor Bueb	'Tiny' Lewis
Peter Collins	Bruce McLaren
John Fitch	Nancy Mitchell
Maurice Gatsonides	Stirling Moss
Anne Hall	Peter Procter
Peter Harper	The Rodriguez Brothers
Mike Hawthorn	Sheila van Damm
Graham Hill	Ken Wharton

INDEX

138